Creative Lettering

Creative Lettering

experimental ideas for
contemporary lettering

Margaret Morgan

A & C BLACK · LONDON

First published in Great Britain in 2009
A & C Black Publishers Limited
36 Soho Square
London W1D 3QY
www.acblack.com

ISBN: 978-0-7136-8247-2

Copyright © 2009 Margaret Morgan
Photographs © 2009 Geoff Morgan

Margaret Morgan has asserted her right
under the Copyright, Design and Patents
Act, 1988, to be identified as the author
of this work.

CIP Catalogue records for this book are
available from the British Library and the
U.S. Library of Congress.

Book design: Susan McIntyre
Cover design: Sutchinda Rangsi Thompson
Commissioning Editor: Linda Lambert
Managing Editor: Sophie Page
Copyeditor: Julian Beecroft

Typeset in Celeste and Gill Sans
Printed and bound in Singapore by
Star Standard Industries (Pte) Ltd.

This book is produced using paper that is
made from wood grown in managed,
sustainable forests. It is natural, renewable and
recyclable. The logging and manufacturing
processes conform to the environmental
regulations of the country of origin.

PAGE 2 Roughs and colour trials for **Tempora mutantur**, see page 64.

PAGE 3 Gloria in excelsis, see page 57.

PAGE 5 **Out of something old**. Letters of different forms and sizes, written in gouache with a cola pen.

CONTENTS

Introduction   7

How to use this book   8

1. Starting off   9
Basic tools and materials: pencils, pens and paper
Easy ways to rule lines for writing

2. Monoline Roman capitals   12
Learning the basics: Form, construction, relative proportions
& letter groups
Working alphabet, linked letters and serifs
Spacing letters, words and lines for legibility
Monoline capitals in action: Exercises, patterns & textures,
different weights and sizes of letter

3. Compressed capitals   28
Change of form to narrow oval: How relative proportions
change, letter groups
Working alphabet, variations, linked letters, slanted capitals
Compressed capitals in action: Exercises, patterns & textures

4. Extended capitals   34
Change of form to very wide: How relative proportions change,
letter groups
Working alphabet, with variations
Extended capitals in action: Exercises, patterns & textures

5. Lower-case letters   38
Expand your understanding of letterforms and increase the
design possibilities
Monoline letters: Form, construction & relative proportions
Alphabets and variations: Classic, Compressed and Extended
Lower-case letters in action: Examples to inspire

6. Next steps   45
More materials, wacky pens, using colour
Specialist materials and tools to extend your capabilities: Pens,
paints and brushes
Pens to make for yourself: Cola pen, rough string pen
More possibilities: Pens made from drinking straws, bamboo,
using wax resist
Colour and how to use it
Coloured papers

7. Putting it all together   62
Exercises and examples of combining the different alphabets
Exploiting textures, contrasting weights & sizes; freeform writing
– using different tools and materials.

8. Design – creativity and composition   70
How a design 'works': understanding what's involved in a good
composition
Developing design skills and visual judgement: useful guidelines,
working intuitively
Thumbnail sketches, cut & paste layouts, centring lines of text
Using 'white space', cropping images for best effect

Conclusion   83

Appendix 1: More about colour   84
Mixing colour and making your own coloured backgrounds

Appendix 2: Simple Japanese-style binding   90

Glossary   93

Useful websites and further reading   95

Index   96

ACKNOWLEDGEMENTS

GWM, not just for taking the photographs but for all the tea and moral support as well!

Grateful thanks to Pilot Pen Co. (UK), the Cumberland Pencil Company and Penmandirect for generously providing materials for photography.

Pater noster, version 4. *Compressed capitals, with some extended letters and other modified forms. Written in black ink with a script (ornament) nib.*

INTRODUCTION

This is a not-quite-conventional look at lettering for anyone of almost any age who has a passing interest in letterforms. They may be young or older, newcomers or experienced calligraphers, teachers or artists from other disciplines. The idea is to move away from the more obviously pretty aspects of hobby calligraphy to experiments using principally capital letters as patterns, texture or explosions of colour, to give a much more general artistic and creative appeal. It is also about learning the skill of careful observation to see what is actually there in terms of letter shapes (not what you think or assume the shapes to be), learning the rules and then knowing how to bend them to suit your purpose.

Work starts with readily available, everyday writing tools and materials; specialist items can be added when the student's skills and ambitions increase. Making your own writing tools from some unlikely materials allows for an exciting exploration of even more different mark-making possibilities.

This is not an undisciplined approach: there is plenty of sound information on letter construction, spacing and relative proportions of letters as the basis for the exercises and experiments which are introduced at each stage. This knowledge is power, because it gives the freedom to be free. Ignorance of rules is not freedom – you won't lose the freshness just by studying the letterforms and putting in some concentrated practice.

However, this book is intended to give a less intense, more intuitive way to proceed with lettering as an art or craft form, with the learning more in the form of 'play'. It establishes precedents that, for the keen student, can later be applied to learning other scripts and developing an individual, personal style. It's also fun to explore just what can be done, moving from the legible to the abstract, in terms of texture and pattern, using those very familiar 26 letters that we take so much for granted.

When you are faced with the problem of nothing in the budget with which to buy special pens for your students, but still have a subject to teach, a fair amount of lateral thinking is required to find easily-come-by materials, as well as an interesting way to communicate the necessary skills.

I found myself in exactly this situation, trying to convey the passion I have for calligraphy and lettering in all its forms to my teaching practice group of self-confessed non-artistic teenagers. Thus I am indebted to them and their unexpected enthusiasm, as well as the numerous individuals (particularly my friends Beryl and Fran, whose views were invaluable) and groups of adult calligraphers on whom I have successfully tried out my theories since.

Margaret Morgan
www.thecalligrapher.co.uk

HOW TO USE THIS BOOK

The whole point of this book is to show that anyone can have fun using letters creatively, with a very small initial outlay. The only real limit is your imagination, so push it to the limit!

There are diagrams that explain the geometrical construction of the letters in 'family groups'. Although these are quite complex, they are intended as a means to an end, rather than an end in themselves. They show the proportional relationship between the letters and aim to help you achieve continuity through each alphabet. The same basic rules apply to all the versions of Roman capitals and, in essence, to the lower-case letters in Chapter 5 as well.

The exercises are intended to be achievable, so the examples that accompany them are not highly finished and some are just working sketches. They have been written mostly using rollerball pens or markers, which are not precision writing instruments and don't always produce the crispest strokes. We might strive for perfection, but for a beginner that is both intimidating and not always possible. If the spirit of the piece is lively and it looks right, 'errors' can be overlooked.

Keep your experiments as a record of what you have achieved; paste them into a scrapbook or create your own book by having the pages spiral-bound. You may prefer to sew them all together in a Japanese-style stab-stitch binding (see Appendix 2, page 90).

Passion, version 2. 'Textured' finish watercolour background (see page 89), worked into with coloured pencils to intensify shadow areas. Lettering written in warm tones of gouache with a cola pen.

STARTING OFF

Writing tools

The photograph shows some of the huge variety of pens and pencils that are available, but keep it simple to begin with – you really don't need any special equipment to get started. Just look around at home to find an ordinary graphite pencil or two, (soft B grades for writing and harder HB or H grades for ruling up), a biro or a rollerball pen. They are all 'monoline' tools and initially ideal for the task; you can add others at a later stage. A clear plastic ruler and a soft eraser are also useful at this stage.

Stationery shops stock pens with different ink colours and point widths, which will help introduce more variety to the letters you make. Look particularly for markers and rollerball pens, but don't ignore the possibility of using coloured pencils, gel markers or wax crayons – but more of these later.

▓ **Your choice of basic materials**

1. *Graphite pencils*
2. *Clutch pencils and leads*
3. *Rollerball pens, with points of different sizes*
4. *Soft eraser*
5. *Plastic ruler, approx 500 mm (18 in.) long*
6. *Marker pens, with bullet tips of various sizes*
7. *Photocopier paper*

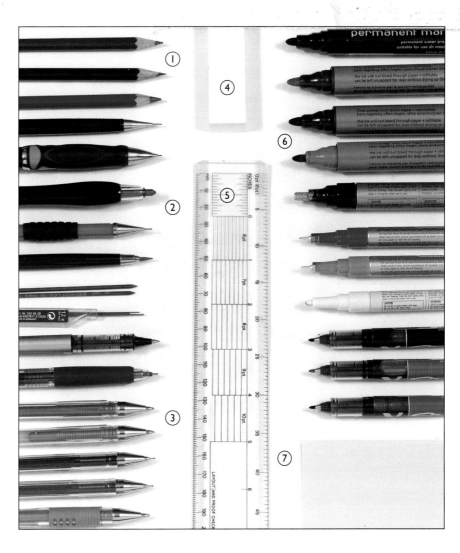

Paper

Photocopier or laser-printer paper is perfect; it's easy to find and not too expensive for the initial practice stages, or for doing roughs for more finished work when your skills and confidence increase. A4 is most common, but A3, if you can get it, is a better size to work on. 80 gsm is a useful weight; when you're working to perfect your designs, it's thin enough to see through the top sheet to the original underneath (see Ruling up to write, page 11 opposite, and Paste-up layouts, page 81).

Sitting comfortably

Try to find a chair that suits the table height, so that you are neither stretching up nor stooping over too much, either of which will be uncomfortable for any length of time. Use a couple of cushions to boost you up, if necessary. Make sure that you work in good light that doesn't cast shadows over the working area (from the left for right-handers or from the right for left-handers), whether it's from a window or a directed desk light.

Working surface

To start with, work on a flat tabletop, with a pad of newspaper underneath the paper you're going to write on. You'll find that this will give a more responsive spring to the writing than a hard surface does; it also protects the table.

Ideally, a drawing board no smaller than 58 x 41 cm (23 x 16 in.), with similar padding taped in position (including a clean sheet of white copier paper or cartridge paper on top), which can be tilted against the table top, will enable you to sit upright and give a much more comfortable writing position. Purpose-made boards can be expensive, but you can find good-sized offcuts of MDF, plywood or blockboard at reasonable cost in DIY stores. Providing that the edges have been cut square, the edges and surface can be sandpapered smooth to avoid snagging clothes.

Another alternative, from kitchen departments of DIY outlets, is a cupboard door. They may have holes drilled in the back for hinges, but those with a smooth, wipe-clean finish and proper edging are perfect.

Ruling up to write: two easy methods

For all your experiments and finished work, you'll need lines to write on. Here are two simple methods, using a sharp 2H pencil and a ruler to prepare your writing lines.

Paper rulers or pre-ruled base templates can be made in advance for any letter height/line space combination you like; they'll save you a lot of time.

At a later date, you could add a T- square to your equipment. With one of these, only one set of tick marks is needed, as the T-square can be moved down the left-hand edge of the drawing board as the lines are drawn.

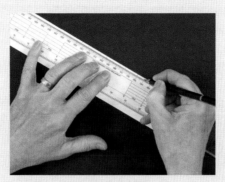

1. Make a paper 'ruler'
Using a narrow strip of paper slightly bigger than the depth of the writing sheet, mark off divisions of 18 mm ($^3/_4$ in.) capital height and 10 mm line space, or 10 mm ($^1/_2$ in.) letter height and 5 mm ($^3/_{16}$ in.) line space (useful sizes for first practice sheets) down one edge of the paper strip.

Mark a measured distance down from the top edge at both ends of the actual writing paper. Align the paper 'ruler' with each of these marks in turn and transfer the letter height and line spaces as a series of tiny tick marks down each edge of the paper. Use the plastic ruler to join up the tick marks and lightly draw in horizontal lines to fill up the page.

2. Make a ruled base template
To avoid having to use this time-consuming method to rule up every new sheet of paper, you can use the same technique described in no. 1 to make a base template of ruled lines. Use a fine black marker to rule in the lines when joining up the tick marks. Slip the pre-ruled sheet under each new piece of paper (80 gsm or less) and the writing lines should be easily visible.

2 | MONOLINE ROMAN CAPITALS

Monoline or skeleton letters are just that, letters made up of single-line strokes using simple tools like pencils or rollerball pens. These letters are the basic building blocks of our exploration: 26 beautiful shapes that can, eventually, be increasingly adapted and modified to make complex and exciting patterns. The classic proportions that make up the letters used at the base of Trajan's Column in Rome are recognized today as being the high point of Roman lettering.

The diagrams on this and the following pages show the basic geometric construction, the underlying structure that contributes to the continuity of form. This is particularly relevant when compressed and extended capitals are looked at in the following chapters.

The alphabet divides into five distinct families based on letter width, with the individual shapes being derived from the circle, rectangle and triangle. The basic construction grid is a circle, set within a square of equal width. If one eighth of the square is cut off both sides, the central rectangle is of approximately equal area to the circle.

The diagrams are complex, but are a means to an end – to help you understand the relative proportions and shapes of the letters – not an end in themselves. Do try the constructions yourself, if that kind of exercise reinforces the principles for you, but being able to write good letters is more important.

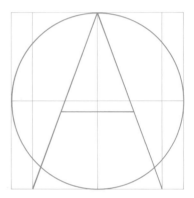

FAMILY GROUPS

Look carefully at the diagrams and relate the details below to the drawn shapes.

Round: O C D G Q are based on the circle and all are of equal area. The straight stem of D relates to the rectangle. O and Q curve slightly through the top and bottom writing lines. The upper and lower curves of C and G do not follow the circle exactly, but are slightly flattened to help the movement of the eye into the next letter.

Rectangular: H A V N T U X Y Z are 'three quarter' letters that fill the inner rectangle and have straight sides and/or diagonals. The cross bar of A is slightly below the centre line, that of H slightly above it.

Narrow 1) E F L K B P R and 2) S J I. Slightly more complicated, 'two storey' letters that occupy half the area of the large square. The diagram shows the top square slightly smaller than, and the bottom square slightly larger than, one quarter of the large square – both are true squares, with the cut off at the sides being $1/16$th of the large square and the curves still based on circles.

1st group: Both cross bars of F are the same width, but the central one is lower than that of E, to balance the white space. The bottom cross bars of E and L are slightly longer. The bowls of B P and R follow the circle, flattened at the middle.

2nd group: The upper and lower strokes of S and J are slightly flattened, as for C and G. The centre of S is not flat; it follows the curves of the offset circles. J can have a shorter tail.

Wide: M W. W is two Vs (two rectangles) side by side. M is not an upside down W, its 'legs' start just inside and finish just outside the rectangle at the corners of the square. The centre section is the same width as V.

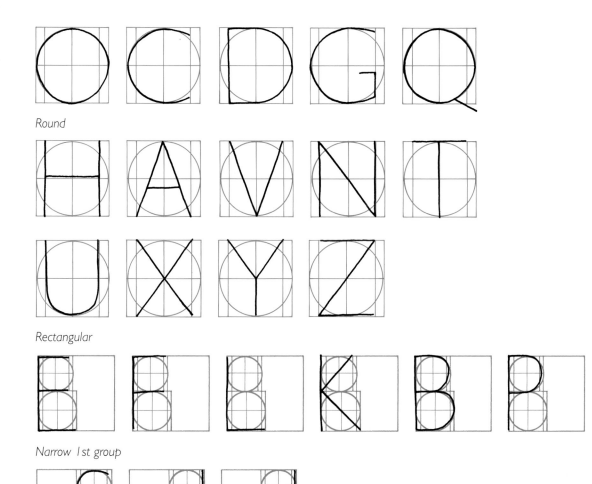

Round

Rectangular

Narrow 1st group

Narrow 2nd group

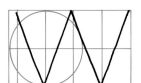

Wide

CLASSIC MONOLINE LETTERS: A WORKING ALPHABET

The letters in all the alphabets in this book are made up of component strokes – verticals, horizontals, diagonals and half-circles, both left and right. This might seem unnecessary, but if you attempt to write these complex forms in only one or two strokes, it will be a struggle and most likely will not give the desired result, particularly at larger sizes. Breaking them down in this way will help you to write them more accurately. Smaller letters may, with practice, be made with fewer strokes, but care is still needed to write them well.

Guidelines, not rigid rules

You may prefer to study the shapes of the letters in the plain alphabet first, then work out for yourself exactly how each letter breaks down into the component strokes, and in which order they could be written.

The easier option is to follow the numbered arrows on the second, smaller alphabet, but even these arrows are only a guide to an efficient way of making each letter, not rigid rules. If after some practice you find another way that works for you, perhaps using fewer strokes, use it as long as the results are good enough.

Writing in this more considered way and taking the extra time to follow the strokes will assist you in the making of good letter shapes, as well as in better understanding the space each letter occupies on the paper. If you intend to learn writing with edged pens in the future, this is a good discipline to learn now.

Use a pencil, black rollerball or fibre-tip pen (at least to start with) for the following set of exercises, but try using coloured pencils or markers, especially for Exercise 3, to add visual interest.

If you have two soft pencils, keep one sharp and let the other become more blunt, to make bolder marks.

TIP

Pencils for lettering

A medium-soft grade (2B or 3B) is ideal to start writing capitals with, as it can make light or dark marks, according to the amount of pressure on the lead. Clutch pencils with 0.5 mm leads always produce crisp lines, but it's a good idea to keep conventional wooden pencils to a reasonable point, using a pencil sharpener or craft knife.

15

Exercise 1: Write the component strokes

Verticals

Horizontals

Diagonals

Half circles

Half circles

a. Use the information in Starting off/Ruling up to write (pages 10 & 11), and rule up several sheets of paper with lines 18 mm (³/₄ in.) apart.

b. Practice the component strokes of the letters (verticals, horizontals, etc.), writing them steadily to get used to the rhythm. Have the pen (and the stroke you are writing) directly in front of you, rather than to one side, so you can see the mark clearly. Move the paper along as necessary.

c. Make each set of strokes close together to begin with, then space them out gradually to actual letter width, as shown in the diagrams above. Don't worry about wobbles

initially; this exercise will train your eye and hand to achieve steady, evenly spaced strokes.

Adjusting pen grip

You may find that to make these strokes evenly you have to adjust your pen grip. It may help to keep the pen shaft quite upright to write verticals and half circles, or to tilt it back towards the knuckles or into the crook of thumb and forefinger for horizontals and diagonals – whichever works best. Experiment until you find a comfortable way of working that suits you.

Pen shaft tilted back for horizontals and diagonals.

Exercise 2: Getting to know the letters

OOCCDDGGQQ *Round*

AAHHNNTTUUVV *Rectangular*

XXYYZZ

EEFFIIBBPPRRKK SSJJ *Narrow*

MMMWW *Wide*

Next, familiarise yourself with the letters by ruling up and writing them out in family groups (as on pages 12 & 13) rather than in alphabetical order, to help you get the continuity of shape within each group.

Using some of the sheets ruled up in Exercise 1, allow one line space (the height of the capitals) between each row of letters.

Work methodically, paying attention to the consistency of form, the order of the strokes and the small details to get each letter just right.

Getting to know the letters, writing letters out in family groups.

'Plotting' letter shapes and position.

TIP

Take the pressure off...

With the added concentration involved here, the temptation is to press hard on the pencil lead, making indentations in the paper.

Hold a ruler in your non-writing hand and press down onto the paper with that – it shifts the balance of pressure away from the pencil point. Try it.

TIP

Plotting letter position

Until you are familiar with them, writing good letters can be difficult, so plotting the shape and position of each letter can be a great help.

Estimate the start and finish of each stroke, the width of the letter and so on, with tiny pencil dots, then join these up (following the order of strokes) to make the letter. With practice, this will become unnecessary, as you'll be able to visualise the letters in your head before you write them. This method is also very helpful with spacing letters accurately when writing words.

Exercise 3: Letters as patterns

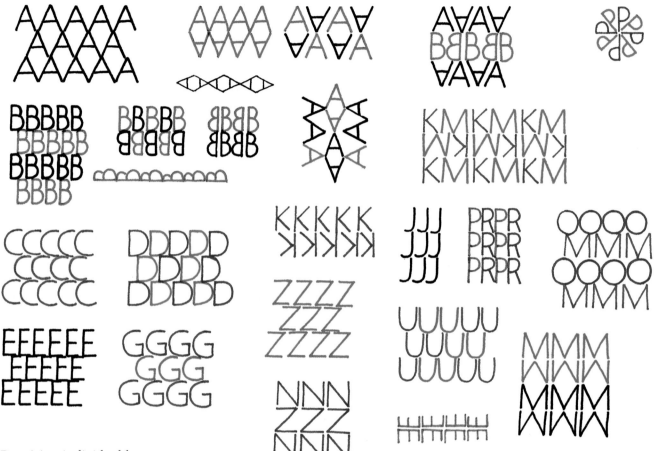

Simple pattern ideas, using letters of the same height and weight.

Practising individual letters, or combinations of one or two letters, can create exciting textural patterns at the same time. Use black or colours as you wish to try the following:

a. Rule up a complete A3 sheet of lines 8 mm (⁵⁄₁₆ in.) apart.

b. Experiment with all the letters, or different combinations, in blocks or strips to see which patterns can be created. Overall textures work best when there is little or no space between letters, lines and words.

c. Turn letters upside down, or back to front, to make a sort of code. See how many permutations you can create.

> **TIP**
>
> - Aim to write the letters well, but don't worry too much as accuracy is not the whole point of this exercise.
>
> - Look for interesting repetition of shapes. Even in simple combinations the rhythms, patterns and the structure or 'scaffolding' that the letters make can be intricate and fascinating. They become more than mere letters and start to take on an identity of their own.
>
> - Some combinations of letters will work better than others. Observe the nature of the patterns – could they be described as calm, busy, spiky, menacing? These qualities could be used effectively at a later stage.
>
> - As your confidence increases, be adventurous and work without ruled lines if you can, which will make the patterns look more lively.

For any sort of calligraphic work, you need to develop an awareness of the space that the individual letters enclose, as well as the space between them, to help you place the letters for optimum legibility, so as soon as you are familiar with the letter shapes and how to write them confidently, it's important to start writing words and to learn the concepts of letter, word and line spacing. The examples given show the ideal standard for maximum clarity and legibility.

What is good spacing and how does it work?

The whole business is about achieving a pleasing visual balance of the space inside and between the letters, avoiding clumps of letters without enough space, and gaps where there is too much.

It cannot be done reliably by any mechanical method. Sometimes only a minute adjustment is needed to make the difference between words that look good and those that do not. There are some useful principles to help you get it right, but there's no substitute for actually writing as many words and letter combinations as you can – it really does get easier with practice.

Tips for good letter spacing

a. Between two verticals (e.g. H E): Approximately ⅝ths of the letter height. This is the key to all the rest, as these letters can almost be viewed as solid blocks of space contained by lines. Follow the

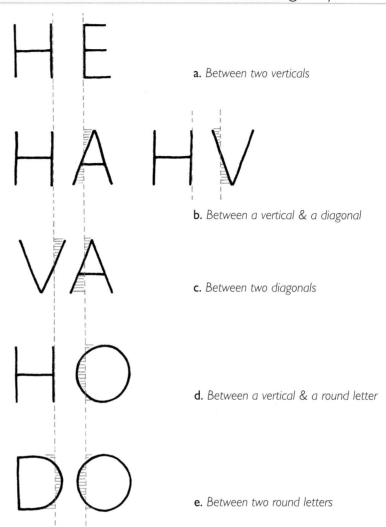

a. *Between two verticals*

b. *Between a vertical & a diagonal*

c. *Between two diagonals*

d. *Between a vertical & a round letter*

e. *Between two round letters*

dotted vertical lines to see how this relates to the following letter combinations.

b. Between a vertical and a diagonal (e.g. H A, H V): Block shape meets larger space at the top or bottom of the following letter. They need to *look* closer than two verticals – whichever way the diagonal lies, it overlaps the hypothetical ⅝ths line separating the two upright letters.

c. Between two diagonals (e.g. V A, M W): When two diagonals occur together, position them so that the area between them appears to be the same as between two verticals.

d. Between a vertical and a round letter (e.g. H O): To compensate for the extra open area around the curve, the round letter overlaps the ⅝ths line.

e. Between two round letters (e.g. DO or OO): These lie closer still, where the curves of both letters overlap the ⅝ths line, to compensate for the space around the two curves.

19

Other examples/tricky combinations

AJ FA KA KE WILL ARK

Spacing problems: Clumps and gaps

Look carefully at these examples below to develop your understanding of how spacing works.

Plotting letters for accurate spacing

As you see, getting the letters spaced accurately within a word can be tricky, so use the tip for plotting described on page 17. It will be a great help in placing each subsequent letter within the word, especially with awkward combinations such as C, K or W followed by an A. This does become easier with practice.

PISCATOR

a. *Not enough space between letters makes for unsightly clumps. This happens particularly with narrow letters like I, J, S, etc.*

P ISC ATOR

b. *Too much space between letters in some places makes for gaps in the word.*

P I S C A T O R

c. *With uniformly overgenerous spacing, letters no longer hang together properly as a word.*

PISCATOR

d. *The shading on this example shows clearly how letter spacing adjustment works in practice. For maximum legibility, letters should look even, right across the word.*

Word spacing

The space between words needs to be more than the space between letters, to make it clear where one word ends and the next begins. It should be approximately the width of O.

Word spacing

Line spacing

For best legibility, the space between lines of capitals is the same as, or slightly less than the height of the letters themselves.

THE QUICK
BROWN FOX
JUMPS OVER
THE LAZY DOG

Line spacing for legibility

Linked letters and serifs

When writing out texts, linked letters are useful to know about as they can save space within a line, if it seems likely to work out longer than you want.

Linking generally requires one of the letters to have a vertical stem, but some slight modifications (e.g. to A and M) may be needed, as well as adjustment of the position of some cross bars. Those shown are some of the most useful; you may find others.

Serifs can be added for visual variety, as appropriate, on most of the letters. At the top they lead the eye into the letter, but as 'feet', they 'ground' the letters onto the writing line. Keep them small and discreet, otherwise they can be distracting.

Some linked letter combinations

Serifs

Exercise 4: Writing words

THYME THYMIAN THYM
MARJORAM MARJOLAINE
SAGE SALBEI SAUGE
MINT MINZE MENTHE
ROSEMARY ROSMARIN ROMARIN
BASIL BASILICUM ALBAHACA

Rule up lines for letters at a cap height of 10 mm (³/₈ in.), with a line space of the same measurement, and write a series of words on a related theme to practise letter spacing.

Write the names of herbs, birds or animals or the members of your family, words in different languages, anything that will give an interesting variety of letter combinations.

Exercise 5: Writing a short quotation

IF ALL THE WORLD WERE PAPER
AND ALL THE SEA WERE INK
IF ALL THE TREES WERE BREAD
AND CHEESE
WHAT SHOULD WE HAVE
TO DRINK?

a. Rule lines 10 mm (³/₈ in.) apart and draw in a vertical line on the left to align your writing.

b. Pick a short quotation, poetry or prose, serious or amusing. This will test your powers of observation and concentration, as you rule up and write the best letters you can, attending to all the details of form, letter, word and line spacing we've looked at so far.

c. If the quote is prose, or if the lines of verse are too long for the width of the paper, think about how to break the lines to retain the sense of the words and where to place the lines in relation to each other. Here the lines are aligned (ranged) left, with the 'overflow' words on the next line indented.

The result should look evenly spaced and easily legible.

Do one version using a pencil or black pen, then try a second with the lines in alternate colours, e.g. red and blue, and compare the different visual effects.

TIP

Ruling up for exercises

Make either a paper ruler or a ruled base template (as page 11) to correspond with the letter height and spacing measurements given for each exercise. Try both methods to decide which one suits you best.

Exercise 6: Writing as texture

IF ALL THE WORLD WERE PAPER
AND ALL THE SEA WERE INK
IF ALL THE TREES WERE BREAD
AND CHEESE
WHAT SHOULD WE HAVE TO DRINK?

This exercise explores the pattern possibilities of words, using a simple texture that still retains some legibility.

a. Rule up lines 10 mm (³/₈ in.) apart and write out the quotation from Exercise 5.

b. Work *without* line spaces, i.e. starting each line directly beneath the previous one, as in the example above. Observe the difference in texture between Exercises 5 and 6 – it should still *look* even, but without line spaces the legibility
is reduced and there is no variety across the piece.

Look where the word spaces occur and how they relate to each other across the piece of work. You may want to adjust some of the line positions to avoid 'rivers' of space running down through the text, or where the same letters recur directly above or at a slight angle to each other – look for T, W, E and R in this example.

Decide how you could alter the line arrangement shown above to improve it.

TIP

Doing revisions or new versions quickly

Layout or copier paper is thin enough to see through, so use this bonus to do revisions or new versions (perhaps in colour) of any exercises that you are not quite satisfied with, without having to start again from scratch.

Lay a clean sheet of paper over the first and write it out again, making any adjustments to the arrangement of the text as you go.

MONOLINE ROMAN CAPITALS

25

Exercise 7: Different letter heights, different textures

IF ALL THE WOR
AND ALL THE SEA WERE INK
IF ALL THE TREES
AND CHEESE AND CHEESE AND
WHAT SHOULD

D WERE PAPER
ND ALL THE SEA WERE INK
WERE BREAD
HEESE AND CHEESE AND CHEESE
VE HAVE TO DRINK?

a. *One colour, with line spaces.*

b. *Two colour, with line spaces.*

c. *One colour, no line spaces.*

d. *Two colours, no line spaces.*

This exercise looks at ribbon patterns and denser textures. Rule up lines alternately for two different letter heights – 10 mm (³⁄₈ in.) for larger capitals and 5 mm (³⁄₁₆ in.) for smaller ones – with a 5 mm (³⁄₁₆ in.) line space.

a. One colour only, with line spaces. Write out the quotation chosen for Exercise 5, with a pencil or black marker of the same point width (or weight of letter). For the second line of smaller capitals, repeat the text to fill up the space.

b. Two colours, with line spaces. Repeat the exercise with pens or pencils of the same point width, but of two different colours.

c. Letter sizes as a & b, one colour, but no line space.

d. As b, but no line spaces.

Observe how:

• the line space makes the eye see the ribbons of letters, but also how the texture is altered by changes in letter height from large to small. Compare with Exercise 6.

• although both sizes are written with the same (pen) point size, the smaller letters look 'darker'.

• the change in colour catches the eye and adds to the contrast between large and small letters.

c. One colour, without line spaces.

d. Two colours, without line spaces.

Observe how:

• removing the line spaces creates a much denser texture using one or two colours.

• without line spaces, legibility is reduced and pattern takes over when all the writing is in the same colour. It looks a little like scaffolding.

• legibility is improved by using another colour for the small letters – the additional contrast catches the eye.

> **TIP**
>
> *If your 'overflow' line of text is short, a useful strategy is to repeat the words (as here) to fill the remainder of the line to match the texture set in the first line of small capitals.*

Exercise 8: More variations of texture, contrast and emphasis

b.

a.

c.

d.

These exercises dispense with both word and line spaces. The examples use just a section of same text from Exercise 5.

a. Write the same text at 10 mm (³⁄₈ in.) cap height, without any word or line spaces. Consider adding small dots or stripes of colour as 'punctuation' between words for verse, or at the end of sentences in continuous prose.

● The texture is even throughout, but the red spots or stripes catch the eye.

b. Same height, change weight on alternate lines. Use pens with different-sized points to change the letter weight from line to line.

● The heavier or bold letters are more prominent, and even the red dots look less obvious.

c. Change weight and height on alternate lines. Write larger capitals (10 mm/³⁄₈ in.) or larger) with a large point and smaller ones (5mm/³⁄₁₆ in. or larger) with a fine point.

● The bold letter texture has the greater emphasis, in spite of the density of the small capitals.

d. Swap the emphasis – write the big capitals with a fine point, the small ones with a big point. Small, bold letters are more emphatic than large fine ones.

● Compare your results with the examples shown here and your

own work from Exercises 5–7, noting how the legibility and the texture alters with each modification.

● Devise your own different permutations to experiment with.

Note:
Writing with a thicker-pointed pen means adjustments have to be made – because of the broader mark it makes, the letters take up relatively more space on the line.

There are more complex exercises to experiment with in Chapter 7, on page 62.

3 | COMPRESSED CAPITALS

A WORKING ALPHABET

This alphabet adapts the standard forms we have already looked at into much narrower shapes, taller than they are wide.

Compressing all the letters proportionally changes the complexion of the alphabet completely. The degree of compression is variable; that shown here is just one example.

ABCDEF
GHIJKL
MNOPQ
RSTUVW
XYZ

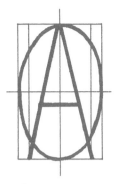

Construction

The relative proportions and the basic construction of all the letters remain the same as those established on page 15, but instead of the circular O that is characteristic of classic Roman capitals, the form is compressed into an oval, which sits within a rectangle rather than a square (see diagram above).

The number and order of strokes for writing each letter shown in the exemplar on this page is the same as before, as are the guidelines for letter, word and line spacing (see pages 19–21).

AABEEEFF

a. *Cross-bar variations*

GHHMMP MD NR NE MRA

b. *Linked letters*

ABCDEFGHIJKLMNOPQRSTUVWXYZ

c. *Slanted caps*

ABCDEFGHIJKLMNPRSTUVWXYZ

d. *Serifs*

Add variety

These 'squashed' forms are particularly useful for getting more words onto a line; they also provide an interesting textural contrast both with the classic forms on pages 16 and 17 and the extended letters in Chapter 4. The linked letter combinations are also effective when space is tight.

Variations in the position of cross bars on A E F H, for example, can also be introduced for visual variety. It is possible to be even more extreme with the degree of compression, but legibility tends to suffer. Slanting (italicising) compressed capitals, which suits the oval letter forms, makes another effective visual change, as can the use of serifs (see examples on pages 22, 23 & 42).

Reminder: **Family groups of compressed letters**

Oval (not round): O C D G Q

Rectangular: H A V N T U X Y Z

Narrow: *a)* E F L K B P R and *b)* S J I

Wide: M W

Reminder: **Ideal spacing rules**

- Letter spacing is about $5/8$ths the letter height
- Word spacing is approximately the width of the oval O, for compressed letters
- Line spacing is the same as the letter height, or slightly less.

Exercise 9: Get to know the new alphabet letter groups

|| (( )) // \\ =ꓑᏰ SS ⊂ *Components*

OCDGQ *Round*

AHNTUVXYZ *Rectangular*

EFIBPRKL SJ *Narrow*

MW *Wide*

Compressed letters: *Component strokes and family groups.*

Rule up for a letter height of 10mm ($^3/_8$ in.) and practise the component strokes first.

These are the same as in Exercise 1, but look particularly for the differences – half ovals, more steeply angled diagonals, shallower central curve of S, etc.

Write out the family groups of compressed letters several times (as in Exercise 2), using one size of pen (or pencil) only.

- Pay particular attention to the new relative letter proportions.

- Leave one line space between the lines of writing.

Exercise 10: Write words, practise letter spacing

NEEDLE NADEL

AIGUILLE AGUJA

PUNTINA NÅL

Rule up lines for a 10 mm (³⁄₈ in.) letter height. Using the same size of pen as in Exercise 9, write out a series of words on any subject, perhaps something suggesting narrowness. Allow one line space between.

● Look for words that have some interesting letter combinations, including words in different languages, to test your abilities.

● Take care with the letter spacing, plotting the position of letters (see page 17). The letters should look evenly spaced for maximum legibility.

● As you work, try out some of the alternative letterforms and cross-bar positions, adding serifs for extra variety.

Exercise 11: Write a quotation

a.

b.

c.

Choose another short text such as the one on this page (*translation*: Times change and we with them), rule up and try writing it out using these permutations:

a. Standard letter, word and line spacing, written at 10 mm (³⁄₈ in.) cap height.

b. Same letter height, with no letter, line or word spacing. This is in two lines, but also try it broken up into five lines, as c. Both are centred (see Design, pages 78 & 81).

c. Same letter height, change letter weight on alternate lines from light to heavy (bold), without any spacing. Write it in one colour first, then again in two different colours.

Observe how:

* linked letters have been used to save a little extra space.

* the use of different forms and cross-bar positions also add to the visual interest.

* texture and emphasis can be changed by variation in spacing, weight and/or colour. Think how this might be used to advantage in finished work.

Turn to Chapter 7, page 62, for more complex exercises, which combine compressed capitals with the classic form.

4 | EXTENDED CAPITALS

A WORKING ALPHABET

Alternative

This time, the letterforms have been expanded into much more generous shapes, wider than they are high. The degree of extension can be greater or less than that shown here. The family groups and proportional relationships are all the same as those of the classic capitals on pages 12 & 13. Some of these extended forms can be more difficult to draw well to start with, and require even more control than classic capitals, so where appropriate the number of strokes involved has been increased. A different form of E is given to add visual variety.

Serifs can be added to compressed capitals, following the examples in Chapter 2 (see pages 22 & 23).

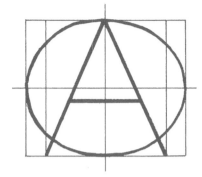

Construction

Alternative

35

Reminder: Family groups of extended letters

Flattened oval (not round): O C D G Q

Rectangular: H A V N T U X Y Z

Narrow: *a)* E F L K B P R and *b)* S J I

Wide: M W

Reminder: Ideal spacing rules

• Letter spacing is about ⅝ths the letter height

• Word spacing is approximately the width of the extended O

• Line spacing is the same as the letter height, or slightly less.

Exercise 12: Write the new alphabet letter groups

Components

OCDGQ *Round*

AHNTUV *Rectangular*

XYZ

EFIBPRKL SJ *Narrow*

MW *Wide*

Follow the same procedure as with the other alphabets.

Rule up lines 10 mm (³⁄₈ in.) apart and try out the component strokes first (looking particularly at the wider half circles and curves, shallower angled diagonals, etc.). These require greater control of the pen and are thus more difficult to make accurately.

Familiarise yourself with these extended shapes by writing out the letters in family groups, before proceeding onto more experimental pieces.

Left: Extended letters:
Component strokes and family groups.

36

Exercise 13: Writing words, practise spacing

PUMPKIN
CITROUILLE
POTIRON
CALABAZA
KURBIS PUMPA

a.

OMNES IGNOTUM
PRO MAGNIFICO

b.

OMNES·IGNOTUM
PRO·MAGNIFICO

OMNES
IGNOTUM
PRO
MAGNIFICO

c.

Quickly move on to writing words and short sentences, as with the other alphabets. Start with words that describe large shapes, to get used to spacing these much more generously shaped letters.

Try foreign-language alternatives again, as they offer both different and interesting letter combinations. This Latin text on this page translates as 'Everything unknown is taken to be magnificent'.

• Follow the same format as previous exercises – first using standard spacing (a), then without (b), then introducing a second colour and change of letter weight (c).

Chapter 7 has a selection of exercises to test your abilities further, combining all three different forms of capitals (see page 64 onwards).

Spacing exercises for extended capitals.

37

5 | LOWER-CASE LETTERS

Once you get the idea of letter construction and the ways of drawing capital letters, it's an easy step to apply the same principles to lower-case letters or minuscules. Getting to know these new shapes will expand your understanding of letterforms generally, and increase the design possibilities significantly.

The construction is very similar to their capital counterparts – a circle within a square and a rectangle of the same area as the circle. Letters are two-thirds the height of capitals, but have ascenders and descenders, that are approximately two-thirds of the x (body) height.

  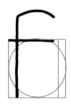 

a. *Round* **b.** *Arched* **c.** *Straight* **d.** *Diagonal*

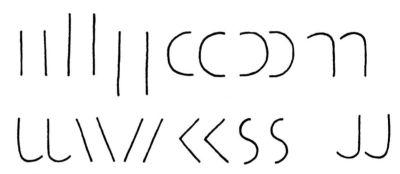

e. *Component strokes*

Basic construction of lower-case letters.

FAMILY GROUPS

Family groups are similar too, but different in some cases:

Round: o c q d e b p and g, which can have two forms; the first variation is made up from a small circle within the ⅛th lines and a lower, oval bowl, which can be open or closed.

Round letters follow the circle, as with capitals. Flatten top curves on c, q & d, and lower curve of p.

Arched: r a u h n m, which follow the top curve of o; u follows the lower curve.

m is twice the width of n.

Straight: i j l t f k. Upper curve of f, lower curves of j, t all follow o but are flattened as previously described.

Diagonal: v w x y z. The base stroke of z is slightly longer than the top one. w is twice the width of n.

S does not quite fit into any of these groups, although the bowls should have a circular feel, with both the top and bottom curves slightly flattened.

Classic

Use the number, order and direction of strokes if you need help to write the letters accurately.

abcdefgh
ijklmnop
qrstuvw

Alternatives, (below)

xyz gy&&

abcdefgh
ijklmnop
qrstuvw

Alternatives, (below)

xyz gy&&

a b c d e f g h i j

k l m n o p q r

s t u v w x y z

g y & &

Alternatives, (left)

Compressed *(left and below)*

Like the compressed capitals, the basis for these small letters is oval. The alphabet given here is of average compression, but it can be made more extreme, as long as all the letters are kept in the same proportion..

Extended *(facing page)*

These letters are based on a larger circle, which gives much more generous forms. Like the capitals, to write the curves of the round letters needs careful attention and control.

Alternatives, (left)

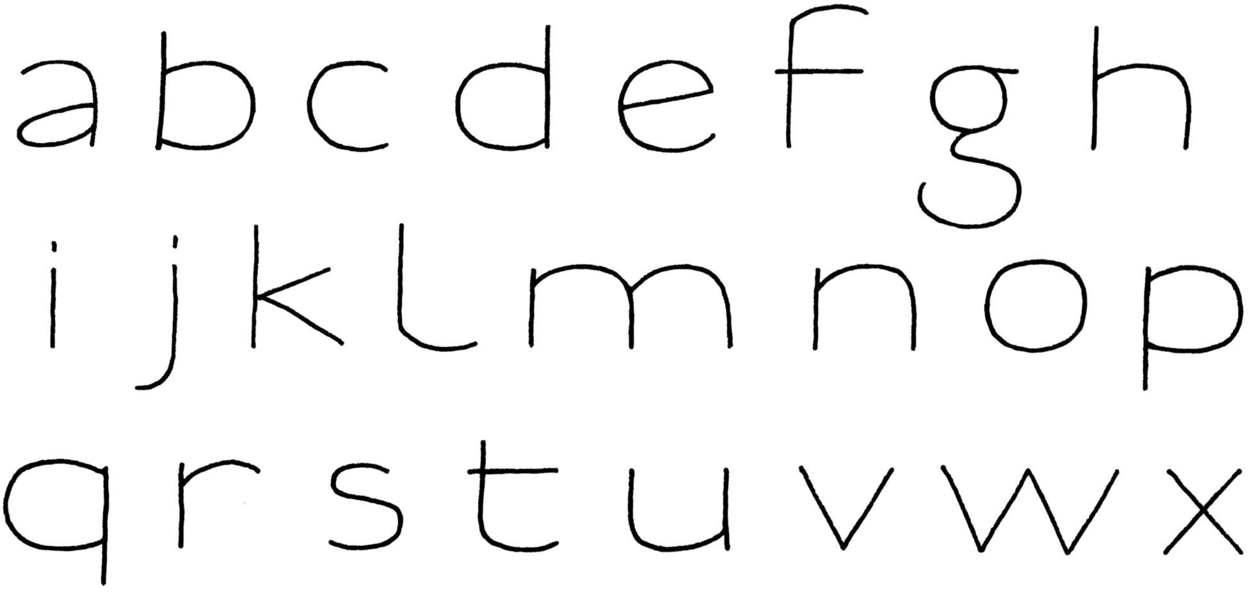

a b c d e f g h
i j k l m n o p
q r s t u v w x

Alternatives, (below)

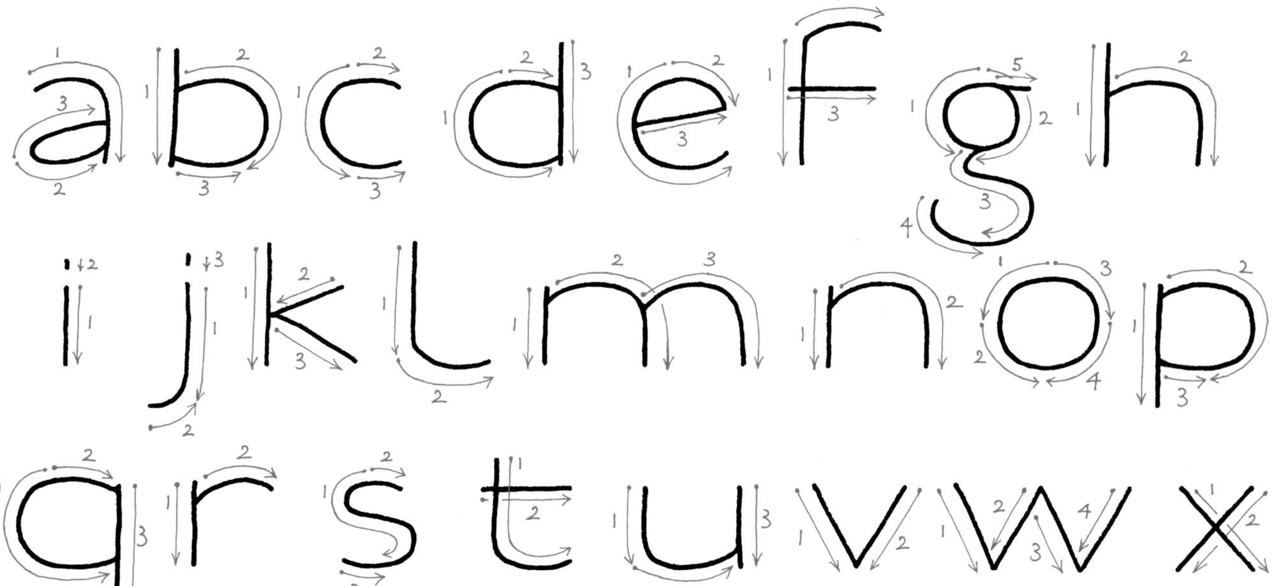

y z g y & &

a b c d e f g h
i j k l m n o p
q r s t u v w x

Alternatives, (below)

y z g y & &

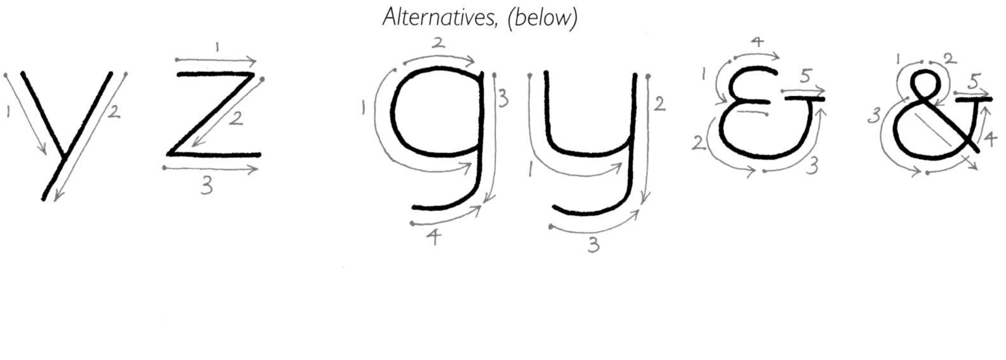

Add serifs for variety

Serifs have already been mentioned in the chapters on capitals; these extra little strokes can be added to give a different dimension to lower-case letters too. Use this example for the classic monoline lower-case as a model for the compressed and extended forms as well.

abcdfhijkl

mnpqrsuv

wxyz

Serifs like these can be added to all three forms of lower-case letters, though not to every letter.

LOWER-CASE LETTERS IN ACTION

Work back through the exercises in Chapters 2, 3 and 4, using lower-case letters instead.

● Practice the component strokes first to get used to the slightly different shapes and rhythms,

then write out the family groups to establish the letterforms in your mind.

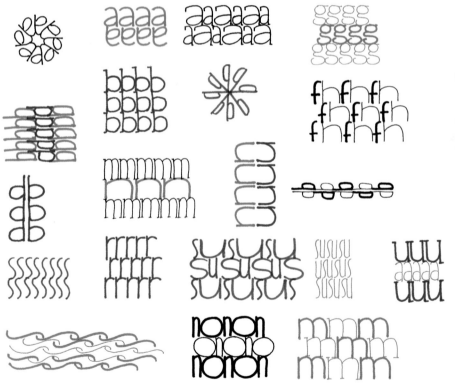

Using single or pairs of letters, first to make simple patterns, then more ambitious combinations.

● Write words, phrases and longer pieces to get the hang of letter and word spacing – the principles are very similar to those for capitals.

● As soon as you are confident, move on to try out more complex combinations of size, weight and form. Turn to Chapter 7 (page 62) for ideas: the exercises outlined will also work with lower-case letters and will give you even more to experiment with. Try the exercises shown opposite and below; page 44 also gives examples to inspire you.

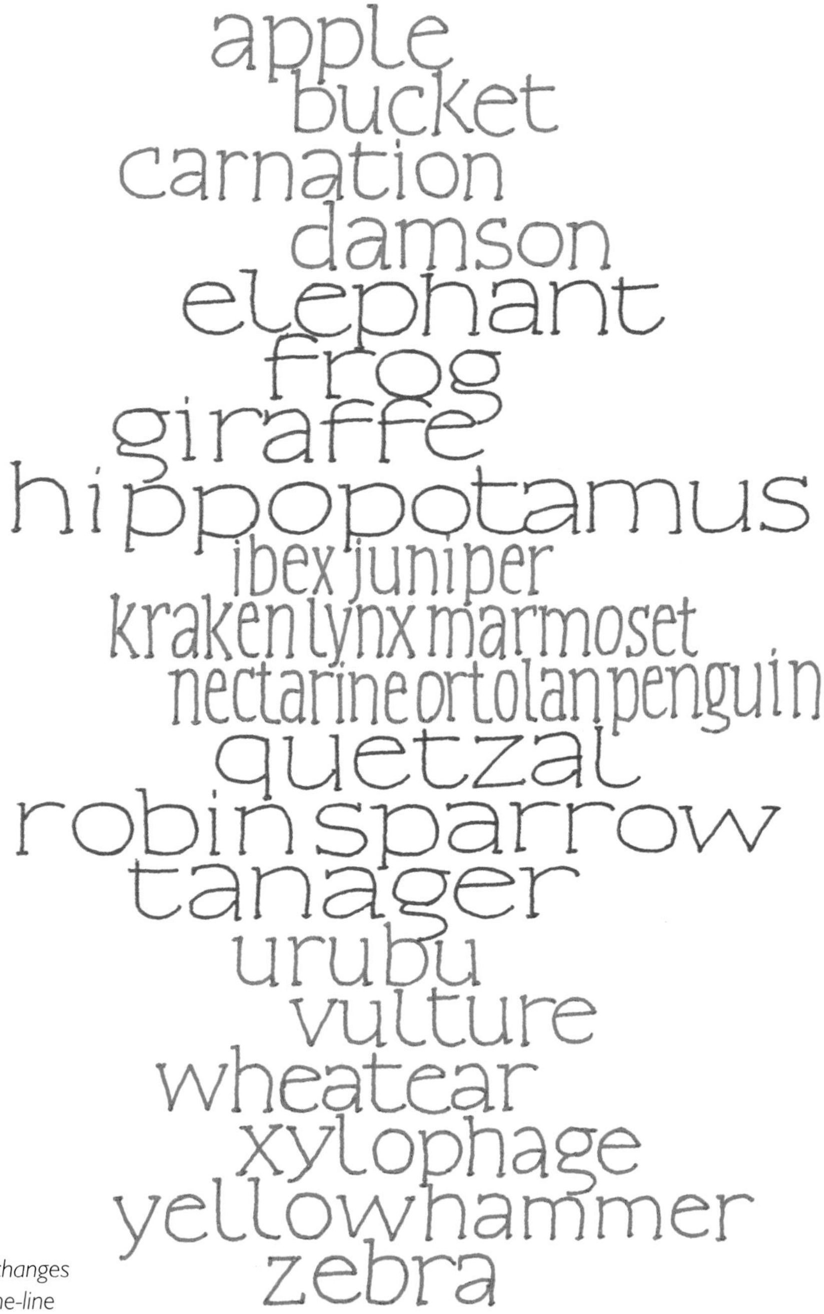

apple
bucket
carnation
damson
elephant
frog
giraffe
hippopotamus
ibex juniper
kraken lynx marmoset
nectarine ortolan penguin
quetzal
robin sparrow
tanager
urubu
vulture
wheatear
xylophage
yellowhammer
zebra

Random alphabet. *Shows simple changes of form and colour, written with fine-line metallic rollerball pens. Extra space on the right balances the weight of text (see Chapter 8, page 70).*

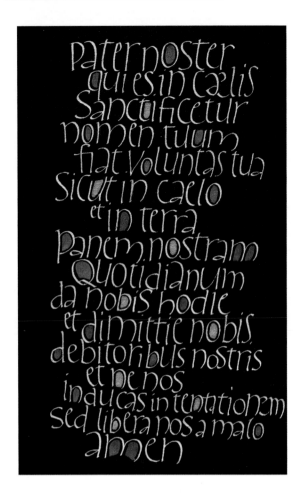

Pater noster, version 1. Compressed letters written in white on black, without ruled lines, and some of the counter-spaces filled with colour.

BELOW ***Das Wessobrunner gebet***. *Freely written colour trial for a finished piece, using two colours of Japanese ink blended in the nib, to write the narrow, serifed letters.*

Das wessobrunner gebet

Ich hörte die Sterblichen staunen am meisten
dass Erde nicht war och oben Himmel
noch irgend ein Berg och Baum nicht war noch
die Sonne nicht schien noch der Mond nicht
Leuchtete noch das berümte Meer da dort
nirgend nichts war an Enden und Wenden

Da war doch der eine allmächtige Gott +

6 NEXT STEPS

MORE MATERIALS, WACKY PENS, USING COLOUR

Specialised tools and materials

Using coloured pencils and markers is fine to begin with, but when your confidence with the letterforms increases, you'll want to extend your capabilities along with your ambitions. At that stage it's worth investing in some extra, more specialised materials.

Key to photo

1. *Selection of monoline dip-nibs and penholders*
2. *Gouache colours*
3. *Watercolour paints*
4. *Mixing palettes and brushes*
5. *Stencil brush*
6. *Gel markers*
7. *Acrylic and non-waterproof inks*
8. *Calligraphy markers*
9. *Coloured pencils*
10. *Thick card and metal ruler for cutting out paper*
11. *Scissors and craft knife*
12. *Selection of white and coloured papers*

Pens

Several manufacturers make monoline dip-nibs (described as Script or Ornament), which have round 'blobs' that deposit the colour onto the paper. These are more versatile than markers, because they can be used with both ink and paint and are also available in quite a wide range of nib sizes.

Calligraphic markers and fountain pens are worth a mention here, but they really fall into a different category, as they have nibs with square edges. In dip-nib form, square-edged pens are generally used for formal writing. All can make marks that are a striking contrast to monoline letters, but writing with edged pens entails a different technique and requires some practice to get used to, which is not within the compass of this book. You may want to try them anyway, but see Further reading on page 95 for useful titles to guide your studies.

Paints

Gouache and watercolour paints come in a wide range of ready-mixed colours in tubes, but you need only a select few to mix a wide variety for yourself (see About mixing paints on page 84). Paint's biggest advantage is that many more subtle colours can be mixed than are available in marker pens. Although the tubes of designer's or artist's-quality paints are more expensive, these will give the best results, so you need only buy a couple of colours to start with, e.g. cadmium red, ultramarine. Mix them to the consistency of thin cream and feed the paint onto the back of the nib (some types have fixed reservoirs which give better ink flow). Most gouache colours are opaque, but watercolours are translucent-allowing the colour of the background to show through.

Mixing paint for writing

Mixing paint
Squeeze out a small blob of paint onto a palette. With a medium-sized brush, add water and mix to the consistency of thin cream, so that it will flow easily from the nib.

Filling the nib with a brush
Feed the paint into nib's reservoir using the brush. Check that the paint flows from the nib onto scrap paper, adding more water if needed. Use the same technique with ink.

Inks

Some stunning colours are available in acrylic and non-waterproof inks, but you do need to wash out nibs and brushes frequently when using them, as they can dry out fairly quickly, clogging the nib and spoiling the flow.

Always wash and dry nibs when you've finished work; if you look after tools in this way, they will last much longer.

Paper

When doing finished pieces of work, you'll need something of better quality and heavier weight than photocopier paper. Most art shops stock white or off-white cartridge and watercolour paper, as well as coloured pastel and cover papers, in both pad and sheet form (see also page 95).

There is a huge range of coloured papers available from art shops and other specialist suppliers (see page 95). Some will supply small sample books of the different ranges of paper they stock, which will help you find your favourites. Look for heavier weights – 160 gsm or more – that give greater stability when folded to make greetings cards or smaller items like bookmarks, and are less likely to cockle when using fairly dilute paint for writing large letters or laying washes (see pages 88 & 89).

Pastel papers like Ingres and Mi-Teintes have an interesting surface texture on one side, and are smooth on the other, either of which can be used. But you need to be aware that some pens will make less crisp strokes on softer-surfaced and rough watercolour papers.

If plain, solid colours don't quite fit the bill for your project, there are several different techniques that can be used to make your own coloured backgrounds; these are described in pages 86–9.

Be aware that some papers are more absorbent than others, and ink will bleed into the surface, giving woolly rather than clean, crisp strokes – this applies particularly when writing with markers – so try them out first.

Extras

You'll need a couple of inexpensive brushes for mixing paint and loading nibs – using a brush rather than dipping straight into the bottle. This avoids ink or paint overload and gives clean strokes.

Multi-welled mixing palettes are available in either china or plastic, but a small white saucer is a good alternative.

Add a large brush, flat or round, if you want to lay watercolour washes (see About mixing paints, page 84). Stencil brushes are worth trying for writing and are relatively inexpensive. The short bristles allow you to make even larger-scale monoline marks quite easily with ink or paint (see *The Dark*, page 69).

A craft knife and scissors are indispensable for cutting out, and the latter can also be used in making your own pens. For cutting out paper accurately to size for finished work, you'll need a metal-edged ruler and a large, thick piece of card for a cutting board.

NEXT STEPS

COLOUR AND HOW TO USE IT

Calligraphy need not be confined to black ink on white paper – colour can enhance the impact of any piece of work, either used in the writing or as the background, in the form of coloured paper or painted washes. It can be symbolic, subtle or bold; used to create a mood or emphasise important parts of the text; it can show harmony or a dramatic, discordant splash. The words or the subject matter that you choose can be used to guide the colour scheme of your piece.

Colour classification

Primary colours: The basics – red, blue and yellow – which cannot be made by mixing.

Secondary colours: Made by mixing together equal amounts of two primaries.

Tertiary colours: Made by mixing together equal amounts of a primary and a secondary colour.

Complementary colours: Directly opposite each other on the colour wheel (e.g. red and green).

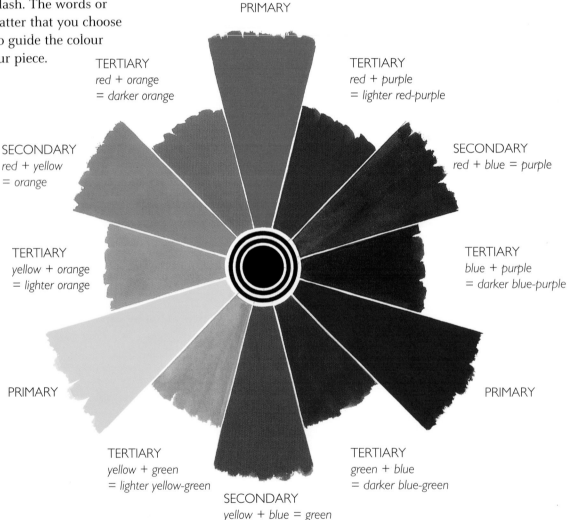

PRIMARY

TERTIARY
*red + orange
= darker orange*

TERTIARY
*red + purple
= lighter red-purple*

SECONDARY
*red + yellow
= orange*

SECONDARY
red + blue = purple

TERTIARY
*yellow + orange
= lighter orange*

TERTIARY
*blue + purple
= darker blue-purple*

PRIMARY

PRIMARY

TERTIARY
*yellow + green
= lighter yellow-green*

TERTIARY
*green + blue
= darker blue-green*

SECONDARY
yellow + blue = green

The colour wheel shows how primaries, secondaries, tertiaries, complementary and analogous colours relate to each other.

Mix any two primaries to make the complementary of the remaining primary (e.g. blue + yellow = green, the complementary of red). Put next to each other, complementary colours cause a visual 'vibration' as equal tones try to neutralize each other. When appropriate, this effect can be used to give real vibrancy to finished work.

Analogous colours: Next to each other on the colour wheel (e.g. red, reddish-orange, orange, yellow-orange). Using this sort of close tonal range of colours gives a look of unity and harmony.

Cool colours: These have a cool blue bias, e.g. blues, greens.

Warm colours: These have a warm red bias, e.g. reds, yellows.

Quick colour exercise

Using gouache or watercolour paints, make your own colour wheel or chart with all the secondary and tertiary colours.

Keep the results of this and the other quick colour exercises together for future reference, with any helpful notes or comments.

Colour schemes

Add contrast *with just a splash of bright colour to catch the eye.*

Add contrast. *Using gold has a similar effect.*

Create unity and harmony *by using a close tonal range of colours, like the analogous ones on the colour wheel.*

Unity and harmony. *Tones of one base colour mixed with white are an alternative.*

Chaos! *Using too many unrelated colours in one piece of work is very distracting. Each one fights for attention.*

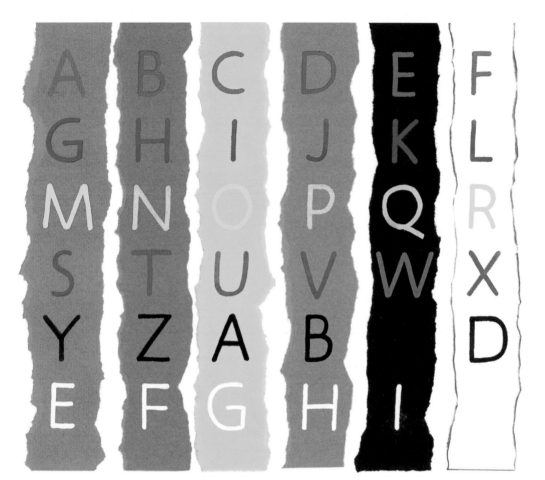

Mid-toned paint colour

Cadmium red

Cobalt blue

Cadmium yellow pale

Oxide of chromium

Ivory black

Opaque white

Colour on colour

When using coloured paint on coloured paper, you need to know how the colours will affect each other, so that the effect can be exploited successfully.

The above examples, using mid-toned paper and paints straight from the tube, as well as on black and white, show how:

• Warm colours (reds, yellows) are more dominant – they 'come forward'.

• Cool colours (blues, greens) recede, are not so dominant.

• Dark on light is dominant, clearly legible. Dark on dark recedes or almost disappears.

• Light on dark is also dominant, also easily legible. Light on light recedes, and with the same colour of paint and paper can almost disappear.

• Colours close in tone appear to vibrate.

Quick colour exercise

Try out these colour experiments for yourself, varying the amounts of the colours in each mix and the coloured papers used. These will be valuable reference in future, so keep them in a sketchbook with a note of the mixes.

More information on colour mixing can be found in About mixing colours, on page 84.

Wacky pens to make yourself

The making and using of your own 'pens' from easily available materials is fun and so cheap that you can make lots. They give both exciting and unexpected possibilities for your lettering experiments.

The following pages introduce several different types of tools and how to make them, with examples exploring their mark-making potential. They are all essentially monoline pens and although some are capable of making multiple lines at one stroke, there is no 'edge' to the nib. The exception is the cola pen, which is capable of making a wide variety of marks using either the pointed tip or the flat blade. Generally they are best used for larger-scale letters, but experimenting with how large or small you can write with each pen could be part of your initial exploration.

All of these tools take some getting used to – unlike pencils and ballpoints, they behave in idiosyncratic and unexpected ways, which is their main attraction. The results are not always predictable or repeatable and some of the pens tend to spatter the writing fluid, especially when used at speed, so wear an overall and cover work surfaces with newspaper to keep things clean.

Take a little time to familiarise yourself with how each of these new tools actually works. Think carefully about how marks can be made and what might constitute the component strokes of the letterforms, including changes from thick to thin, where appropriate. In this way you can evolve your own alphabets, which use each tool's special characteristics to best effect.

Try them also for loose, expressive drawings that could be incorporated into a finished piece of work. Work through some of the exercises in the earlier chapters using these experimental tools, and compare results with the monoline pens and pencils.

Most of these pens can be used with ink or paint, but whichever you use, you will need to wash and dry them thoroughly both during and after writing so that the colours always remain clean. Even though they cost so little, it's worth keeping them in good working condition.

Making a cola pen

This ingenious pen is very easy and quick to make. The 'nib' gives tremendous scope for different kinds of strokes and letter shapes.

When the writing tip splits, as it will after a while, just cut a new nib and replace the old one.

MATERIALS

- Empty soft drinks can
- Craft knife
- Scissors
- Length of dowel or garden cane approx 8 mm (¼in.) diameter and 14 mm (6 in.) long (or use a pencil instead)
- Pencils: 3B (soft) for initial drawing, 2H (hard) for transferring shape to card and metal
- Tracing paper
- Thin card
- Masking tape

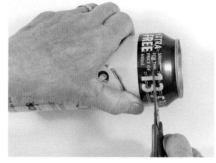

1. Trace the nib template from the drawing (below) with the soft pencil onto tracing paper. Turn the drawing over and use the hard pencil to transfer the shape onto thin card and cut it out with a craft knife or scissors.

Cut off both ends of the can – pierce the metal first with the craft knife, then insert the scissors and cut round carefully, taking care of the sharp metal edges. Use the scissors to cut open the body of the can and dry the inside with a paper towel.

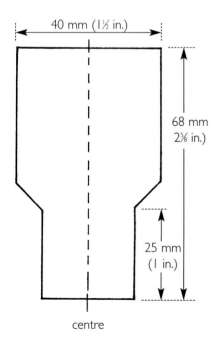

40 mm (1½ in.)

68 mm 2⅝ in.)

25 mm (1 in.)

centre

Template for cola pen nib, with measurements.

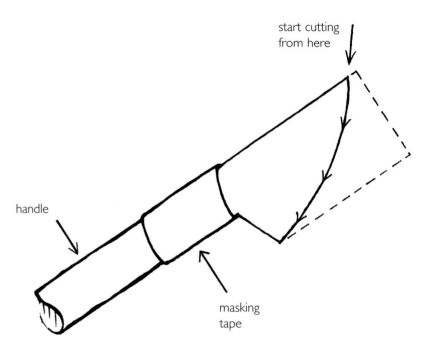

start cutting from here

handle

masking tape

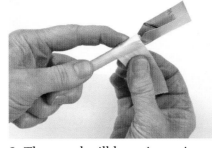

2. Flatten out the can by curving it backwards. Place the card template on the metal and trace round it with the hard pencil (or an old ballpoint pen). This makes an indentation in the metal, giving you a cutting guideline. Cut out with scissors.

3. The metal will be quite springy, but fold the cut metal shape down the centre line to make the nib. Wrap the narrow end around the dowel, using masking tape to keep it in place.

4. Cut the nib as shown, starting from the top edge (see also diagram). The fold might need opening slightly before it works properly, and it will also need de-greasing.

Apply a match flame to the writing edge for a second or two, then plunge it into cold water. Any rough edges can be smoothed with glass paper. Now you're ready to write.

Finished cola pens from above, below and the side.

Mark-making with cola pens

MATERIALS

- Either: Ink (black or coloured) or
- Gouache or watercolour paint (see mixing instructions on p. 46)
- Paintbrush and palette or saucer
- Paper

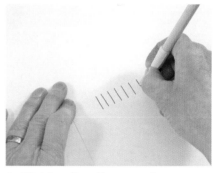

1. Use a brush to load the nib with ink or pre-mixed paint. The amount needed will depend on whether you are going to write broad or fine lines – you'll only find out how much by trial and error.

2. Writing fine lines needs a normal pen grip, but with the pen barrel held upright so that only the tip of the nib touches the paper.

Move the pen slowly towards you, supporting the weight of your hand on the little finger.

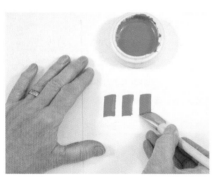

3. Making broad marks needs a different grip. The pen barrel can be tilted either towards or away from you (try both ways), so that more of the flat edge of the nib is in contact with the paper. Make the marks slowly, allowing the paint to flow in a uniform stroke width. If you rush, the width will be different, so allow time to practice.

4. Write with speed. Letters written with greater speed and freedom of arm movement still need a certain amount of control, but the process is more dynamic. It is also likely to produce paint spatters especially when trying to write flourished letters like this – but that's just part of the fun!

Writing words with a lot of ink or paint in the nib gives other possibilities. Either blow the excess ink away from/across the image to make strands of colour, or fold the sheet of paper back on itself to 'squash' the image out into blots. Cola pen letters can also be written very tall and thin, or be used with masking fluid (see page 67).

These pens will not last very long, but they are infinitely replaceable. The tip will split after a while. Either trim it back with scissors or make an entirely new nib.

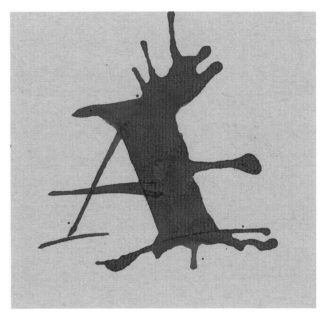

Excess ink blown can be blown into strands.

Folding the paper and excess ink (top) or paint (below) will make blot patterns.

Making a string pen

MATERIALS

- Rough garden string (natural fibres work best, but try synthetic fibre too)
- Scissors
- Masking tape
- Ink or paint (gouache or acrylic)
- Paintbrush and palette or saucer for mixing paint

I. Cut the string into 10 cm (4 in.) lengths and bind the centre section with masking tape, to stop the string unravelling and give you something more substantial to hold when writing. This gives two usable 'nibs'.

2. Fray both ends of the string, opening out the strands to make a sort of brush. Trim the ends flush with a pair of sharp scissors.

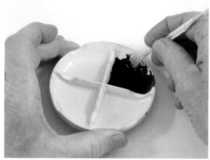

3. Mix some gouache to a medium creamy consistency. Hold the pen on the tape grip, load one end with paint (or ink) and wipe off the excess on the side of the palette. Too much paint will make for a rather solid letter.

4. For writing, the pen should be held vertically over the paper (which can be on either a flat or slightly angled work surface – see Starting Off, page 16). Writing needs to be done in bold, confident strokes with a fairly free arm movement; resting your wrist tends to restrict this freedom.

Writing with string pens

The strength of the mark depends on the amount of paint or ink on the writing end. Only a little is needed to make all the separate strands show up clearly. The pen needs to be reloaded at least every other letter, or more often if the writing is very large.

The strands will get saturated after a while and clump together, so it's a good idea to have several pens made up and ready to use. Rinse out and dry off the strands on paper towels after use.

Gloria in excelsis. Written with black ink. Stroke density depends on both the stiffness of the string and the amount of paint or ink used. Experiment to find the best combination.

SOME MORE IDEAS

1. Plastic drinking straw pen

Make cuts about 25 mm (1 in.) down from one end of the straw to create 'bristles' about 1–2 mm (about $^{1}/_{16}$ in.) wide. Use a sharp craft knife for the first few cuts; the rest can be snipped with nail scissors.

The bristles will vary in width, as it gets progressively more difficult to cut narrow strips as you work around the straw's circumference.

NB Take care when using the sharp blade on the first cuts.

Using a straw pen

The 'bristles' are not very flexible and the mark-making is extremely unpredictable. The shredded ends need frequent reloading as the plastic does not absorb ink or paint. Don't shake or wipe off what looks like excess, or there will be no liquid left to write with.

Freely written letters in bold, confident strokes (as with the string pen) can show great vitality. The irregularity of strokes and spatters from the strands are part of the charm.

Mark-making with a straw pen, using acrylic ink on coloured paper.

2. Bamboo pen

Trim off about 150 mm (6 in.) from a garden cane (any circumference) with a hacksaw. Sand the rough edges smooth with sandpaper. To write, dip the end frequently into ink or fairly dilute paint.

The shaft of the pen needs to be held vertical to keep the whole of the circumference on the paper.

Written with a bamboo pen.

3. Wax resist

Sharpen the end of a white wax candle or crayon to write letters or words, then add a colour wash of ink or paint over everything. The waxy letters resist the colour and will show up white.

Wax-resist letters.

4. Paint straight from the tube

Judge how much paint to squeeze to the open end of the tube and write directly onto paper.

'Broken' letters can be made by using the tube's edge to shape the colour, but fine strokes are not easily achieved.

Letters written using paint straight from the tube.

5. Gel markers

These crayon-like tools, which come in bright, pastel or metallic colours, are best used for strong, bold letters. Their broad tips are not really suitable for making thin strokes.

Enjoy the experimentation!

Fruit tower. *Freely written trial, using gel markers on coloured paper.*

61

7 PUTTING IT ALL TOGETHER

TIME TO EXPERIMENT FREELY

Studying, practising and becoming familiar with all the alphabets in Chapters 2 to 5 will have been time well spent, as now it's time to push the boundaries further still. Your knowledge will enable you to play with more extreme experiments in contrasting textures, working with the minimum of spacing to combine alphabets or particular aspects of each form into more complex patterns. Pattern is more important here than legibility. It's also a chance to try out some of the new tools and papers mentioned in Chapter 6 for some light-hearted projects, like making greetings cards, gift wrap or bookmarks for friends or family.

There are so many more permutations to explore – writing 'freeform' without lines, following curves and changing the size of letters within each line, combining large open letters with tightly compressed ones, mixing capitals and lower-case letters, using different tools for contrast in style of mark-making, adding serifs.

Layering text is another avenue to follow (see pages 72 & 73), writing words horizontally or diagonally over a base layer of text written vertically – or any combination of those – with different weights, sizes, form and/or colour to give a rich, dense texture.

If you haven't done so already, make up new paper templates to rule up for a range of different letter heights. There are some ideas on pages 63–6 using a text long enough to show the patterns. They will also work equally well with lower-case letters, which will produce quite different textures.

Work all the exercises with the variations given, but try as many other possibilities as you can think of (there are ideas in the exercises in other chapters). Compare the results – work out how emphasis or contrast can be achieved. Is it only by weight, size or colour of letters, or a combination of these? Your conclusions will prove useful when you read Chapter 8.

Exercise 14: Compressed caps, combinations and extremes

Pick one short text for this exercise, which leaves out word and line spaces. Write with fine or large round points and use alternative forms, cross-bar positions, etc. for visual interest. The French quotation used here translates as 'After the things that are most necessary for life, there is nothing more precious than books.'

a. Same height, change form. Write out alternate lines of compressed and classic capitals of the same size, using two colours. The eye registers the classic caps first, the dense texture of the compressed caps afterwards, in spite of them being red.

b. Same colour, change form and height. Make up paper ruling templates for different letter heights (e.g. 10 & 5 mm (³/₈ & ³/₁₆ in.)) and write the text in alternating lines of large compressed letters and small classic capitals. The emphasis is still on the classic caps, their weight and density contrasting with the thin, compressed letters even though the latter are larger.

c. Really push the boundaries of compressed capitals. See how tall and narrow you can make them – the taller they are, the narrower they become. Alternate these with lines of smaller, classic capitals to make a really big visual contrast; the second colour, slightly offset, adds another dimension to the pattern.

a. Two forms, two colours, same letter height.

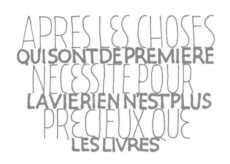

b. Two forms, one colour, different letter heights.

c. Extreme contrast in one and two colours, the second colour offset to the right.

● Compare carefully the textures and patterns that you have created. Note how varying the form, weight and height governs the number of words on each line and appears to alter the emphasis or visual impact of the words.

● Variations can also be manipulated to create blocks of text of the same width. Centring lines of text (see Design, page 82) can also be put to good use here.

Exercise 15: Extended caps, combinations

• In your practice work, experiment with changes of weight or height of letters and colours too, restricting the choices to one or two differences for each piece of work.

• Try out some interesting combinations of different letterforms with other writing tools or media – refer back to the ideas in exercises 6, 7, 8, 11 and 14 and techniques in Chapter 6 for ideas.

Extended capitals combined with compressed (above). *Letters written with coloured pencil, spaces filled in with a second colour.*

Tempora mutantur (right)
Letter patterns can be vertical as well as horizontal. Written in gouache with script (ornament) nibs on a watercolour wash.

Exercise 16: More variations

These can be done either with capitals or lower case – b. uses both in one. Try each exercise first with same-size points, then introduce a broader point for one of the changes in form.

a. Write any circular letters (O C D G or Q) in extended form, to contrast with the rest written in compressed letters. The eye sees the holes first, then registers the rest of the text.

b. Extended letters can also be introduced wherever they work within the pattern, as opposed to just using the circular ones, as these don't always occur where you would like to have them!

Write the extended forms with a finer point in a different colour to the rest of the text.

c. Change form, weight and colour on alternate lines. Some liberties have been taken with the lower-case letters to make them appear the same height as the caps. The texture of lightweight caps contrasts with the tight-packed lower-case letters; the contrast is emphasised by the difference in colour. Try the same exercise in one colour and compare results.

These exercises are based on using the same letter height (with minor exceptions in b., but there are many more variations to try. Work to a definite plan for each new piece, using one or two variations rather than trying too many alternatives in one example, which will be visually confusing.

a. Circular letters extended.

b. Other extended letters used within the text, as well as circular ones, using two weights of letter.

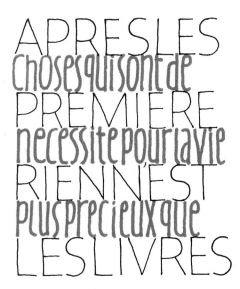

c. Change form, weight and colour alternately.

Exercise 17: Freeform, with compressed capitals, variations

Pater noster, version 2. Varied amount of compression. Different cross-bar position and varied forms for variety and contrast. Written with related colours of gouache and monoline nibs, using a coloured pencil for background (see Specialist materials, page 45).

Exercise 16a used very compressed letters combined with extended forms. Now try this.

● Lightly draw a couple of curved or wavy lines freehand with a 2H pencil, to show the 'movement' of the text. Start to write, allowing the letters to rise and fall, tilting the uprights slightly to left or right (according to the slope of the line) and allow the piece to evolve line by line.

● If you still need the security of a line to write on, continue to put these in lightly. Left to trail off, the lines could always be incorporated as part of the overall design, helping to balance the shape of the piece.

● Before doing a finished piece, any necessary refinements to the composition can be made on tracing or other thin paper. Lay the first version under a fresh sheet of paper and write it again, adjusting the lines backwards or forwards as needed.

● Try a version in tones of one colour; or one with two different colours on alternate lines; or one with colour shading from dark to light (or vice versa). Experiment!

When you have completed this group of exercises, go back to those in Chapters 2, 3, 4 and 5. Decide how you can use what you have learned there, as well as Chapter 6's exploration of colour and unusual tools, to re-interpret the earlier exercises into more colourful and visually exciting examples.

Look at the pieces shown here as a springboard to further your own experiments.

Pater noster, version 3. Written with masking fluid in a cola pen, with textured wash background (see *Make your own coloured backgrounds*, page 89).

Cityscape. Uses broad marks with dilute gouache from a cola pen for the 'buildings', combined with graphite watercolour pencils for the shadows. Letters are written with different point sizes of rollerball pens.

Baa baa black sheep. *Letters scratched through a layer of black oil pastel to reveal a patchwork of colours beneath.*

Best wishes. *Design idea for gift wrap or greetings card, using different tools and letterforms. Close-cropping emphasises the pattern.*

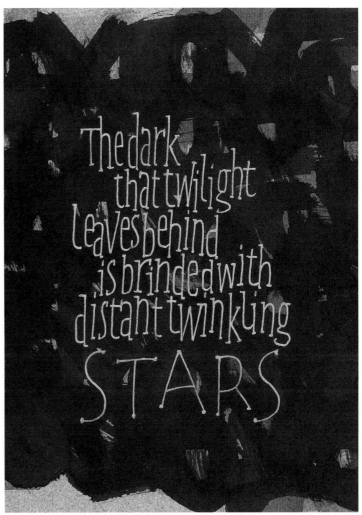

The Dark. *Idea for layered work, using stencil brush, black ink and fine silver marker on textured dark-grey paper.*

'By passion'. *Letters written in gouache with a cola pen on stretched, colour-glazed calico panel.*

8 DESIGN – CREATIVITY & COMPOSITION

UNDERSTANDING THE IMPORTANCE OF DESIGN

You will find that certain of the concepts introduced in this section have already been covered less formally in earlier chapters. This section deals with the production of more 'serious' pieces of work with longer (or several) texts, where words and their meaning are as important as the patterns or textures that they make. It aims to show how the composition of this kind of piece can be crucial to its success; how form, spacing and colour can be used to interpret the mood or feeling of a text; why a design can be said to 'work' (or not); and it gives simple principles and techniques to help.

There are some simple tasks to try which will ease you into the concept of composition, without having to worry about words.

First, you'll need these:

MATERIALS

- A sheet of A4 black paper
- HB pencil
- Ruler (metal if possible)
- Craft knife
- Cutting board or thick card

1. With the pencil, mark divisions of 8 x 25 mm ($^5/_{16}$ x 1 in.) along the short edge of the paper, then mark 3 x 25 mm ($^1/_8$ x 1 in.) down the long edge. Rule up the 24 squares.

2. Divide up the remaining area of paper into 22 strips of 245 x 10 mm ($9^3/_4$ x $^3/_8$ in.).

3. Cut out the squares and strips carefully, with craft knife and ruler.

Quick exercises in design using abstract shapes

Placing one black square on the paper creates a relationship or tension with the space around it, and even with the edges of the paper. Each additional square breaks the old relationship and makes a new one. When arranged in a definite order they look like stepping stones, making a strong line of force or direction, so do consider carefully where each new square is placed.

Try the following, making small pencil sketches of each composition (and what you intend it to represent) for future reference. The photographs suggest some starting points for your experiments:

a. Create a mood or feeling – e.g. calmness, laughter, energy, sadness, fear. Start with three squares, but use more if you need to.

b. Introduce a circular movement to the arrangements, and compare with the results from a.

c. Use some of the strips (at full size or smaller) to see if you can create the same moods with straight lines.

Using black squares to illustrate 'calm'.

Using black squares to create 'energy'.

Using black squares to create 'energy', with circular movement.

'Energy' using black strips has a different feel.

Bear in mind

● Repetition, the basic element of composition, is a rhythm of marks (or blocks of letters/text) across the paper. Too much repetition can be visually boring, so consider introducing:

● Contrast, a change of rhythm needed at the heart of the composition. Think how this might be achieved – will it be sharp or gradual?

● A line of squares can be livelier than a solid line (see photos above), but it doesn't have the same strength of force or direction. Try it out and compare the results.

Experiment with as many variations as you can think of to achieve the above, sketching the results and noting what they represent; these will be useful for future reference.

His Dark Materials

His Dark Materials. *Putting principles of design and layout into practice, using a sketchbook for thumbnail sketches and colour trials (see also pages 78–81).*

RIGHT **His Dark Materials**, *the finished piece: Written in three layers of colour, without any ruled lines. Fine yellow pen-written capitals over the blocky, dark-blue brush-written letters, with a dilute blue wash in between. Text from* Paradise Lost *by John Milton.*

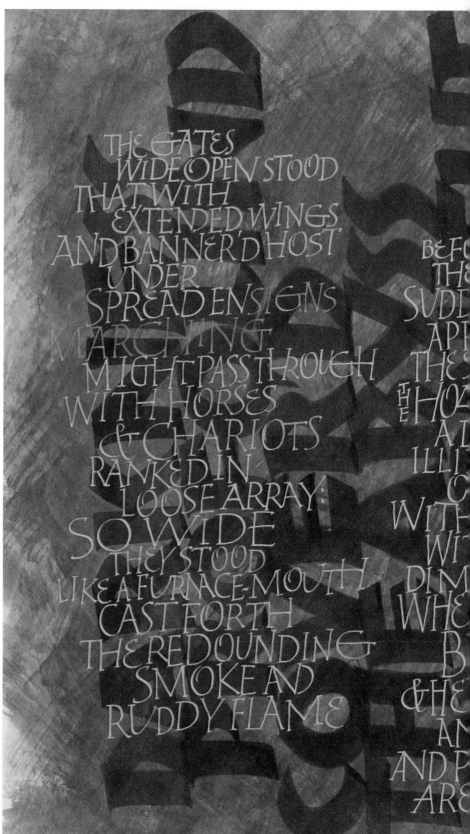

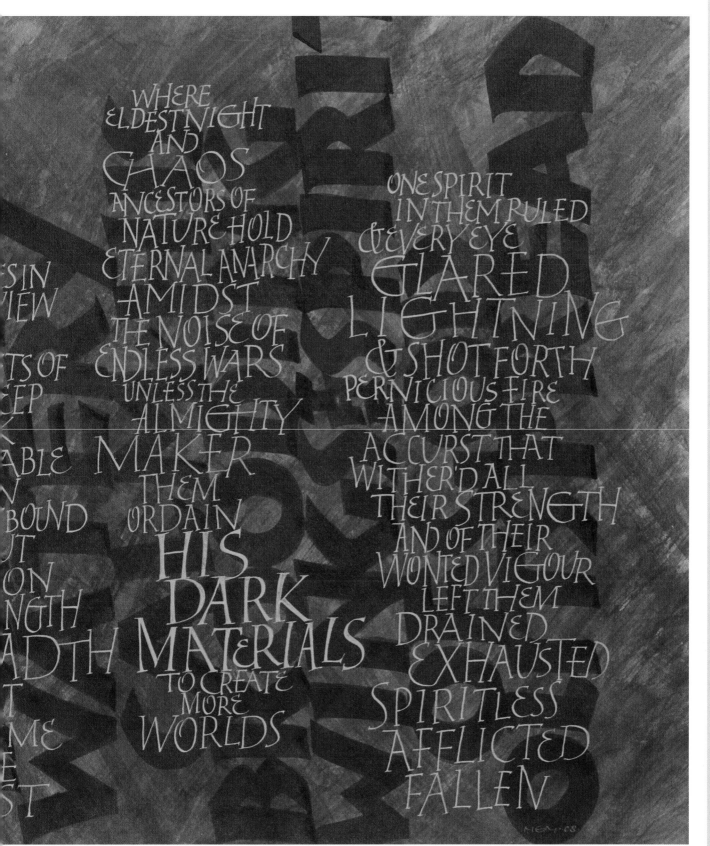

WHAT IS 'GOOD' DESIGN?

How can you judge whether a piece of lettering 'works'? What criteria can you use to analyse the success or failure, in terms of composition? Could you answer those questions? Perhaps not at the moment. Many people say that they are not creative, or have trouble thinking up and developing their own ideas, but this skill and judgement can be learned.

Look at this example (*facing page, left*). The text was written directly, without any sketching-out of ideas or planning first. The resulting layout has rather too much variety in letterform, weight and colour; it is not balanced, has no clear focal point, and the piece is cropped too closely to the text, giving the words no room to 'breathe'.

Close-cropping can be effective where pattern is more important (see the examples in Chapter 7), but in this context more space would be appropriate. The lack of a focal point and sufficient space around the words directing the eye into the composition is distracting and rather claustrophobic.

However, the piece could be used as a starting point for further development. There are plenty of ideas to choose from, but they would benefit from some careful selection first.

The same text has been used here (*facing page, right*), but this version can be said to 'work' for the following reasons:

1. The size, weight, proportion and colour of the letters and background are visually attractive.

2. The arrangement (composition) of the lines of text has been planned carefully so that it is balanced.

3. The composition leads your eye into the piece, and there is enough space around the text to encourage the viewer to explore the detail as well as the overall texture.

This doesn't happen by accident or magic. It has been achieved by a series of experiments, starting with little sketches before the finished piece was begun, in order to make conscious choices about the best

size, weight, proportion and colour of letterforms, making a cut-and-paste layout to choose the most pleasing arrangement of lines and using cropping strips to decide the optimum amount of white space around the text (see Making a paste-up layouts, pages 80 & 81).

The text has a powerful message, but while strong reds and browns perhaps spring to mind as a first choice, it was decided to use a less obvious colour – soft-green pencils on a pale-green textured paper – to reflect the author's ethos (she was an 11th-century German abbess). The slightly stiff pen-written letters of the layout (see Making a paste-up layout, pages 80 & 81) were exchanged for more freely written, multi-stroked letters to try and convey the vitality of the words.

TIP

Developing visual judgement

- *Use the black squares and/or strips to learn how to 'place' the elements without having to worry about words. Refer back to page 71 and your own work to remind yourself of the procedure.*

- *Look at examples of calligraphy or painting that you like and analyse why you like them, why they work. Conversely, choose an image you don't like or that you think doesn't work, then list your reasons.*

- *Keep all of your work, even the pieces you are not pleased with. These will provide valuable exercises in analysis, to figure out what you feel is wrong with them and how they might be improved.*

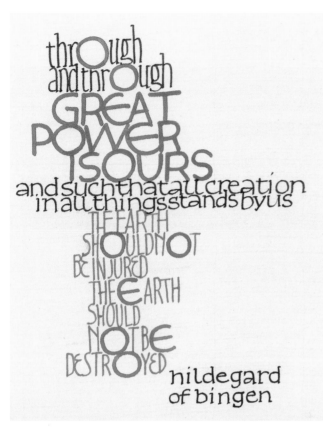

Not entirely successful. Too many differences in form, weight, size and colour.

More successful. Simpler, with restricted choice of form, weight, size and colour.

A PRAGMATIC APPROACH

This will be of most help if you are not sure where to begin and prefer to be given easy steps to follow that will get you started. There is no right or wrong way to approach design, more a way of finding a method of working that suits you, possibly a combination that uses both the pragmatic and the abstract/intuitive.

It's tempting to miss out the preparatory stages and start by working straight onto expensive paper without much thought beforehand. But not knowing if the writing has been started in the right place on the paper, or whether the colour, size and style of lettering will look right, it can be very frustrating. Time spent thinking about your ideas and composition first will eliminate these difficulties. In this regard, the exercises you have already done with paper squares & strips should have helped establish some ideas.

Design is very subjective and personal and the elements are variable, so it pays to experiment and then analyse the results carefully, so that you learn to develop your own judgement.

Starting with a rough design will help to make everything fit and work. Even though the emphasis may be more on texture or pattern than legibility, it's still important to keep an eye on the effectiveness of the composition.

First ideas are not always the best ones, so don't be afraid to work on them, by changing the style of lettering and layout, or trying a different approach, until you feel you have something that works.

The next part of the chapter outlines step by step the way to plan and achieve a successful piece of work.

Formulate your plan, stage 1

Use this checklist to help sort out your ideas and note down the answers as you work through it.

1. How big is the piece going to be? The size of the letters will be one of the deciding factors, as will the size of paper that you want to use.

2. What – or who – is the piece for? You may get some clues here that help with the following questions on text, letterforms, layout, colour, etc.

3. What text (words) shall I use? Poetry, prose, something of my own?

4. Is it going to be formal or informal? This has a bearing on question 6.

5. Shall I use capitals or lower-case, classic or one of the modified forms? A mixture?

6. Decide what (if appropriate) is the most or least important element in the design. How can size, weight and colour be used to deal with this? See 'Emphasis'.

7. How should the text arranged to best effect? Don't forget to allow space around the text – it's also an important part of the composition.

8. Shall I use colour? Which colour(s)? This could be symbolic, used to create a mood, a favourite, or just what you have available!

9. What materials? Coloured paper, paint, markers, coloured pencils, or a mixture? Perhaps a specially made background (See Make your own coloured backgrounds, pages 86–89).

Having got the answer to these questions, there are three more concepts to consider. They are all ideas that have already been introduced in the exercises and examples earlier in the book:

Emphasis
Use the size, weight or colour to pick out the most important words or elements in the design. Think about how to achieve this – perhaps tall thin letters or small heavy ones (thin strokes/thick strokes) – it's likely to be different in each new composition.

Variety or contrast
These two are essentially used for the same ends, to gain and retain interest in your composition. As for 'Emphasis', consider changing the height, weight or form of the letters, e.g. using extended round letters within a composition of compressed letters (see pages 65 & 66) or inverting the text as a sort of mirror image. The 'colour' or density of the text can provide variety – think of newspaper typography, where headlines contrast with subheadings and text. Actual colour can also be used to introduce variety.

Remember, you have to work out and choose just how much variety or contrast is right for each piece of work. Too many differences are distracting.

Spacing
Using standard, increased, reduced spacing – or even none at all – between words and lines which will affect the visual texture.

Quick checklist of contrast possibilities

Open (e.g. Classic or extended) / **tight** (compressed)

Thin stroke width (light) / **thick stroke width** (bold)

Exaggerated horizontally / **exaggerated vertically**

Letters right way up / **letters inverted**

Planning, stage 2

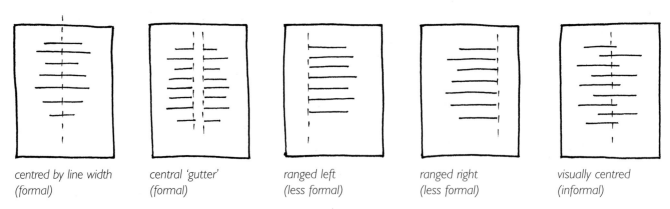

centred by line width
(formal)

central 'gutter'
(formal)

ranged left
(less formal)

ranged right
(less formal)

visually centred
(informal)

Placing and aligning the text *– showing lines of text of varying lengths. Dotted lines indicate axis of alignment. Note how and where the text is placed in each rectangle, allowing white space round it.*

Having worked through stage 1, some ideas have probably started to take shape in your mind. The simplest way to visualise them is to make small pencil sketches or thumbnails, roughly indicating words or phrases by scribbling in lines (or even rough letter shapes) that represent the approximate weight, size and spacing for each element of the design, in relation to each other. Set them within a rectangle that is about the same proportion as the paper you intend to use (if it is already cut to size). The diagrams show some possibilities for different arrangements.

Don't be afraid to play with textures and combinations of forms, as well as placement within the space.

Formats, margins *– showing lines of text of roughly equal length.*

Symmetrical

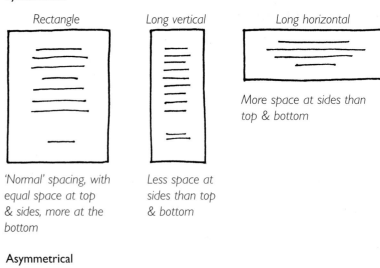

Rectangle

Long vertical

Long horizontal

More space at sides than top & bottom

'Normal' spacing, with equal space at top & sides, more at the bottom

Less space at sides than top & bottom

Asymmetrical

Long vertical

Long horizontal

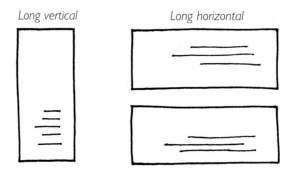

Note how the final shape of the piece reflects the amount of text being used, and also that the margins ('white space') should roughly balance the amount of text.

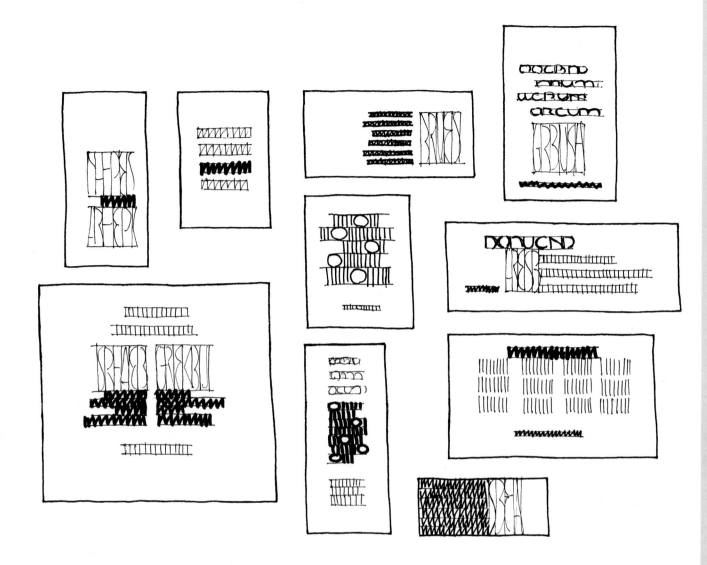

Emphasis/variety/contrast. Shows changes of weight or size of text using double or darker lines to indicate heavier, bolder letters; tall thin lines for large compressed letters; circles for extended letters; line spacing or none, as appropriate.

Remember

These little sketches are only to help in visualising your ideas on paper. They are an abstract rendition of the composition to which you give real shape when working with the words at actual size. You can alter things at any stage, both here and when making the paste-up layouts.

MAKING A PASTE-UP LAYOUT, TRANSLATING THUMBNAIL SKETCHES TO ACTUAL SIZE

Choose a thumbnail sketch that looks promising and work it up to actual size by making a paste-up layout. This is a useful technique to learn as a beginner; it works at all levels, both for little practice projects as well as larger, more complex pieces that you may want to tackle in the future. It will help you make decisions about the design – whether it works or not, as well as what might resolve the problems if it doesn't.

Initially, it is not easy to understand exactly how to translate the thumbnail sketches into full-size layouts. Use them as a basic idea, a guide to help you choose the right size and weight of lettering, but be prepared to modify them as necessary at each stage. If some parts of the composition don't appear to look right, you need only rewrite those parts and substitute them on the pasted-up layout.

It's quite all right to make changes – that's the main point of the exercise. Until you have the right sizes and weights of writing, it's difficult to make the best decisions about placing and spacing. Keep the first version so that comparisons can be made between each variation. Every time you work on layouts this way it will further develop your creative judgement.

A window mount (mat) can be added, with the opening cut to the area decided on at stage 4.

You'll need:

MATERIALS

- Several sheets of layout or photocopier paper (A3 or larger)
- Scissors
- Adhesive tape or repositionable glue
- Tracing paper
- Cropping strips of black or dark paper, approx. 8 cm (3 in.) wide and 76 cm (30 in.) long
- Markers, pens, ink, paint, etc. that you wish to use

See the completed piece on page 75.

TIPS

- *If in doubt about the size of paper to use, always pick a larger sheet than you think you need, as this will allow for much greater flexibility in choosing margins for the finished work.*

- *Follow the sense of the words, as well as your layout, when choosing line breaks.*

- *Photocopy, or scan and print your original lettering (stage 1) before you cut it out. Use this to make up an alternative paste-up, and compare the two to see which works best, without having to write everything out again.*

- *If you find it difficult to translate lettering sizes and weights from thumbnails, draft the layout in pencil first, at approximately full size. It doesn't remove the need for a paste-up – you will most likely still want to adjust things, and that is the most efficient way to do it – but it will be easier to see what works and to manage the move from tiny sketch to full size.*

1. Rule up and write out all the text, gauging appropriate size(s) and weights from the thumbnail sketch. Leave space around and between each line for cutting out. Work in black ink or paint (or pencil) to start with.

2. Cut everything out with scissors and assemble together (following thumbnail sketch) on a fresh sheet of paper. Tack each piece in place with repositionable glue or adhesive tape. Adjust line spaces to take account of ascenders & descenders, or the lack of them. Work visually rather than mechanically, so that it *looks* right.

3. Lay tracing paper over the paste-up. This disguises the patch marks and helps you to assess the layout's effectiveness. Use a T-square (if you have one) to check that lines are level. Rewrite if necessary, making changes to size, weight or position, repeating steps 1 to 3.

4. Make a ruling template (see page 11) to transfer line positions to a clean sheet of layout paper. Lay this over the paste-up from stages 2 & 3 and rewrite, refining letter quality and spacing as you work. Without the distraction of patches it will be clear whether the spacing and position look right. If not, rework stages 2 to 4 as needed until you are happy with it.

5. Use cropping strips on the final version from stage 4 to decide on the margins. Move the strips to assess the effect that more (or less) white space has on the area of writing. Mark in the chosen position in pencil on the layout.

6. Colour trials. An important final stage – you can't assume that your choice and balance of colours will be just right without trying them out before you start the finished piece (see Colour on colour, page 50). It also helps to get used to working with paint on a slightly textured surface, a different experience compared to ink on layout paper.

Doing the finished piece

Use the ruling template made at stage 4 to mark the position of each line on your chosen paper. If the layout is aligned left, you need only draw a vertical in the appropriate place (worked out on the paste-up) and rule up the lines from that – it is not crucial if any of them run out slightly longer when written.

For asymmetric layouts, measure the start and finish of each line on the paste-up, mark these on the paper and rule up between these marks with a sharp pencil, using a light touch. This gives exactly the right length of line on which to write. Centred layouts are dealt with in a similar way, (see also Tip: Centring text *right*).

It's important that you try to retain the freshness and vitality of the lettering from the early stages in this process. All too often the result can end up being rather lifeless from trying too hard to 'get it right'. A little extra practice to boost your confidence before starting your finished piece will make a big difference, knowing that you can match letter shapes and line lengths accurately.

Centring text at layout stage, matching centre and baseline marks.

TIP

Centring text

a. *Rule up, write text and cut out as paste-up layout steps 1 and 2.*

b. *Measure the length of each strip of text, marking the centre with a pencil.*

c. *Rule up writing lines on base paper, as stage 4, with the addition of a vertical line at the centre of the layout.*

d. *Match up base lines and centre marks for each line of text and tack in place.*

For ruling up and writing finished work, follow description in 'Doing the finished piece'.

Moving on

As your abilities increase, you may find that the process of ruling lines for writing and making paste-ups may not always do what you want; the result might look too stiff or formal. It may be risky, but at this stage it is worth experimenting with ruling up only the first line, or writing without any lines at all, just letting it 'flow'. You still need to do these roughs on layout paper first, but you can cut and paste any corrections or alterations over the top, as needed.

Go back through the exercises in the first few chapters and see how you can adapt those ideas into visually interesting and larger-scale finished pieces, using the additional knowledge on colour and design from Chapters 6, 7 and 8.

CONCLUSION

These pages contain just a few of the exciting and visually creative possibilities; the examples are really just a taster. Expand your horizons by looking at art forms from other cultures in Europe, the Middle East and Asia, to see what inspiration can be gained from painting, sculpture, textiles – even graffiti – from the past as well as current trends.

Nor should you overlook the inspiration to be found in the huge array of type fonts that are available now. Many of the traditional favourites (e.g. Garamond, Baskerville) were derived from the writing styles in old manuscripts; modern script fonts have their origins in calligraphic pen and brush lettering styles. Work out how you might adapt and translate the ideas into new, personal scripts.

Note down all your ideas in a sketchbook for future reference, but, above all, keep making marks and exploring your own new ways of making them. The only limit is your imagination and the time you have to spare.

The apples of autumn. Colour sketch for a finished piece. Letters written with coloured sumi ink, over a strip of colour wash, on pale-cream textured paper, evoke the time of year.

ABOUT MIXING PAINTS

The theory that all colours can be mixed from three primaries is a simplification. To mix pure, clean colours, you need to know the 'bias' of the primaries you are going to use. This selection of six gives two of each primary colour, one each of warm or cool bias.

Mix *with* bias for the richest, truest secondary colours. *Against* bias, the secondary colours will be duller and more subtle. The quantities of each primary used in the mix will also influence the result. Experiment with mixing lots of colours, both with and against bias, making notes on how the results were achieved (i.e. the quantities used in each mix) for future reference, so that they can be easily repeated.

Quick colour exercise

Work through the colour mixes with and against bias mentioned here, but experiment with the amount of colour in each mix. Always note down quantities used so that you can repeat specific mixes without difficulty.

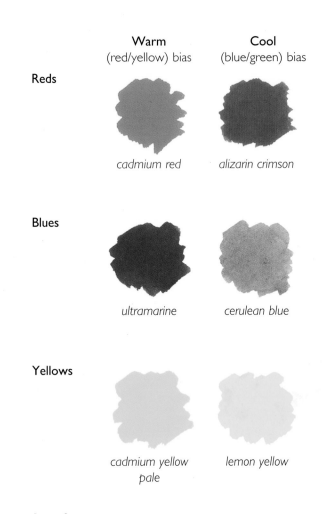

	Warm (red/yellow) bias	Cool (blue/green) bias
Reds	cadmium red	alizarin crimson
Blues	ultramarine	cerulean blue
Yellows	cadmium yellow pale	lemon yellow

Bias of primaries.

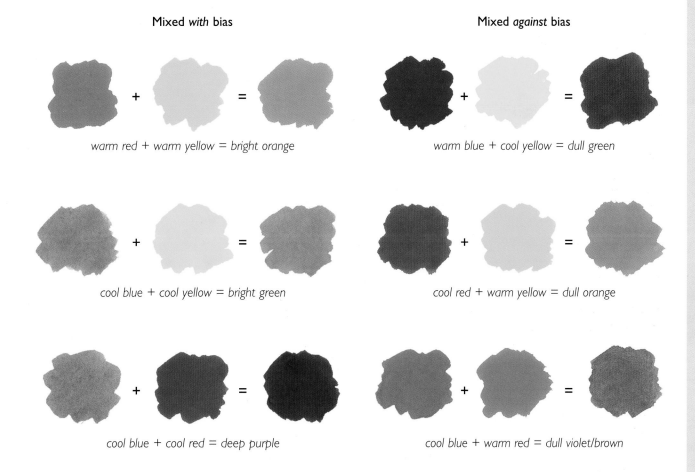

Mixed *with* bias

warm red + warm yellow = bright orange

cool blue + cool yellow = bright green

cool blue + cool red = deep purple

Mixed *against* bias

warm blue + cool yellow = dull green

cool red + warm yellow = dull orange

cool blue + warm red = dull violet/brown

Mixing colours. How the bias of primaries affects secondaries. Mixes based on equal quantities of each colour.

Blacks and whites: Mixing shades, tints and tones

Adding varying amounts of black to colours makes different shades. For warm shades use ivory black; lampblack yields cooler shades.

Mixing zinc white with any colours will give clean, lightfast tints – useful when you want to make a series of graded tones of the same basic colour.

Permanent or opaque white is useful for white lettering on coloured paper.

MAKE YOUR OWN COLOURED BACKGROUNDS

There are several simple techniques you can use to make your own interesting backgrounds for lettering projects.

1. With soft pastels

MATERIALS

- Soft pastels (the chalky type, not oil pastels)
- A craft knife
- Cartridge paper (or any smooth or slightly textured white paper
- Cotton wool
- Spray fixative for pastels

Use the knife blade to scrape the pastel onto the paper, then rub and press the powder gently into the surface with a pad of cotton wool. Experiment with single or blends of two or more colours.

Spray lightly with fixative before writing. Gouache or ink in dip-nibs, felt-tip markers or coloured pencils will give better results than rollerball pens, which tend to clog up with the pastel powder.

Finished pastel background, ready to write on.

2. Watercolour washes

Heavier weights of watercolour paper (300 gsm and more) generally do not need to be stretched before laying coloured washes. However, lighter weights (and cartridge paper) do need to be stretched before painting, to stop the paper cockling as it dries.

MATERIALS

- Watercolour or cartridge paper
- Tubes of watercolour paint
- Brushes and saucers or palettes for mixing
- Sponge
- Gummed paper tape, 40 mm wide
- Wide, soft watercolour brush
- Piece of clean plywood board (an offcut from a DIY store will be fine). Must be larger than the paper, plus the tape that holds it in place
- Food wrap (cling film) for textured finish

Stretching paper

1. Hold the paper under running (cold) water, wetting both sides evenly. Drain off excess water and lay the sheet onto a clean plywood board that is larger than the paper. Blot the surface with a dry (or damp) sponge, without scrubbing, which will spoil the paper.

2. Cut a strip of gummed paper tape for each side of the paper. Using a wet sponge, damp one strip at a time and stick down onto the board, overlapping the edges of the paper by about 10 mm (³⁄₈ in). When all the strips are in place, lay the board flat and allow the paper to dry out completely.

Sticking tape in place over the edge of the paper.

a. Plain wash

Mopping up the excess paint from the last stroke.

Mix the paint with water to the desired depth of colour and use the wide brush to apply the paint onto the pre-stretched paper, with the board tilted at the top about 40 mm (2 in.).

Pull the brush steadily across the top of the paper, without stopping until you reach the other side. Repeat the process, with enough paint to give a 'puddle' at the bottom of each stroke. Overlap this line each time to blend the strokes together, until the whole sheet is covered. Resist the temptation to patch any areas that might have been missed!

Mop up the excess paint from the last stroke with a dry brush or kitchen paper and leave the board flat to dry out, as before.

b. Two-colour wash

You can use the same technique to make a two-colour wash. Lay the first colour (as described previously) as far as the middle of the paper. Turn the board round and use the second colour to work to the middle again, overlapping the two colours where they meet, letting them bleed into each other. Control the blending of colours by tipping and turning the board. Leave the board flat to dry completely.

c. Variegated wash, wet-into-wet

Tilt the board as before and wet the stretched paper with clean water, using brush, sponge or a spray bottle. While the water soaks in for a minute or two, mix up two or more colours in separate palettes or saucers, then load a large brush with the first colour and apply to some areas of the paper, leaving other areas white. Repeat the process with the other colours, allowing them to mingle. Leave flat to dry out.

For brighter colours, add more paint to the mixture in the palette. To tone down the colours, add more water. If the result isn't to your liking, before the paint dries, hold the board under running water and use a sponge carefully to remove the paint. Leave it to dry out before starting again.

d. 'Textured' finish

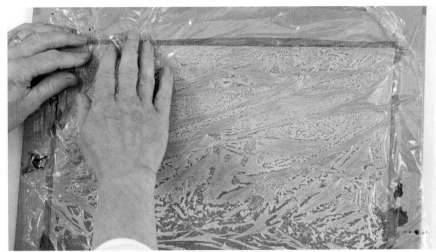

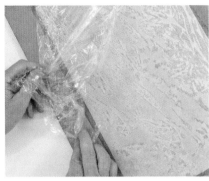

Revealing the 'textured' result.

Stretch paper and lay a background wash – single, two-colour or variegated – as described.

While the paint is still wet, lay a piece of food wrap (cling film) over the whole of the painted area, pulling the film together slightly into 'clumps'.

Leave flat to dry. Remove the film to reveal an interesting pattern, which is like a cross between tie-dye and batik.

The results are always un-predictable and unrepeatable. (See 'Pater noster, Chapter 7, page 67).

APPENDIX | SIMPLE JAPANESE-STYLE BINDING

This four-hole stab-stitch style of binding is a useful way of collecting together your ideas, experiments, working sketches, colour trials, etc.

Choose a consistent page size, so that the book can be made up of single pages of work, or like an album, with smaller pieces stuck onto sheets of paper that are the same size.

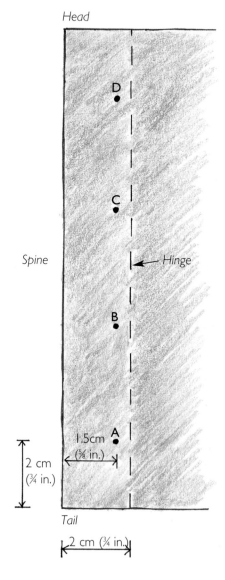

Diagram 1: Position of hinge and stitching holes on front cover.

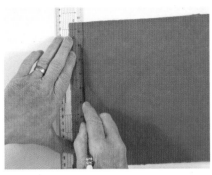

1. Make the cover. Cut paper to match the size of pages with a turn-in allowance of approximately 5 cm (2 in.) at both fore edges. For the front cover, measure and mark lightly with a sharp pencil 2 cm (³/₄ in.) in from the left-hand (spine) edge to make a hinge (see diagram 1). Line up the ruler on the two marks and use the tea knife or bone folder to score the fold line.

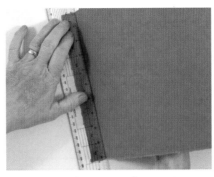

2. Fold the hinge and turn-in. Keep the ruler in place and use the knife to ease the cover from underneath to establish the fold. Score and fold the turn-in on both covers in the same way.

3. Collect all pages, together with front and back covers and knock them gently to align them accurately. Wrap the whole book in several sheets of clean paper to protect the covers, then attach the bulldog clips to keep everything in place. Measure 2 cm (³/₄ in.) from the top and bottom edges of the book and 1.5 cm (⅝ in.) in from the spine edge. Mark with a sharp pencil (as diagram 1), then divide the remaining space into three, marking these other sewing points.

4. Make sewing holes. With the thick card beneath the back cover to avoid damage to the work surface, use the bodkin to push right through all the pages. Some force may be needed if the book is a thick one; you might need to tap the cork end of the bodkin with something heavy like a hammer or weight.

5. Sewing. With plenty of thread in your needle (about three and a half times the length of the spine) start sewing. Put the needle in from the spine edge, a few pages in from the front cover, coming up through hole B, leaving enough thread for tying off when the sewing is complete. Make the first stitch in at C, then follow diagram 2 (on page 92) to complete the sewing.

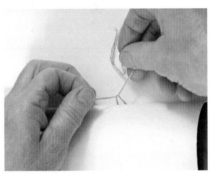

6. To finish, remove the clips and paper and push the needle back through at B, to come out *inside* the book, where the entry stitch was made. Rethread the needle with the loose ends from the first stitch and take them back inside the book. Open the pages where both ends of the thread are, and knot the two ends securely, pulling the knot firmly into the spine. Trim off the excess with scissors.

SIMPLE JAPANESE-STYLE BINDING

91

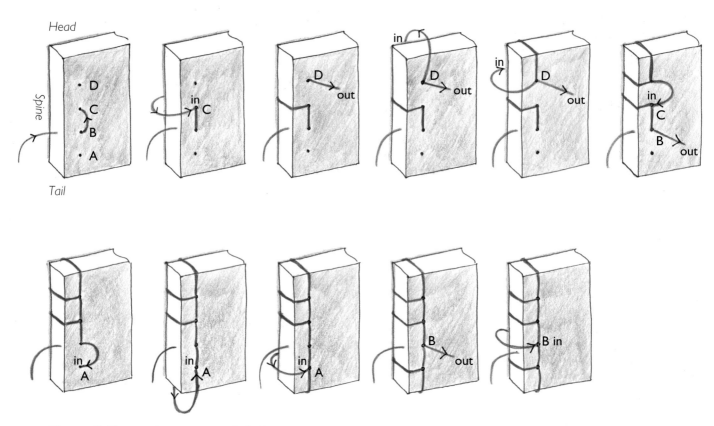

Head

Spine

Tail

Diagram 2: The complete sequence of stitching.

1. In at spine, come out at B, into C and out at the back of the book.

2. From the back, make a loop round the spine and go back in at C.

3. Make a stitch at the back, coming out at D.

4. Make a loop over the head and back out at D.

5. Make a loop over the spine and come out again at D.

6. Take the thread back in at C, make a stitch at the back and come out at B.

7. Make a stitch in at A and come out at the back.

8. From the back, loop over the tail and in again at A.

9. Make a loop over the spine and go in again at A.

10. Make a stitch at the back, to come out at B.

11. Loop over the spine and in at the back of B. Bring the needle through to the inside, close to the entry stitch (photo 5). Finish as photo 6.

NB At each stage of the stitching pull the thread tight, but without pulling the loose end of thread into the book or buckling the block of pages.

If you are unsure of the stitching procedure, make a dummy booklet from scrap paper and practice the stitching sequence on that before embarking on the real thing.

It's easier to make several thin volumes rather than one very thick one, as it is quite hard work to push the bodkin through too many sheets of paper as well as the covers.

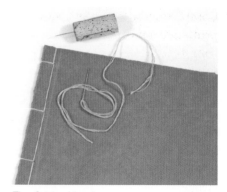

The finished book

GLOSSARY

Analogous colour Colours next to each other on the colour wheel.

Ascender Part of the lower-case letter extending above the *x* height.

Baseline The line on which letters are written.

Bleed Occurs when the paper surface absorbs ink or paint.

Body height The main part of the letter. See *x* height.

Bowl Curved letter strokes, enclosing a counter.

Bone folder A flat piece of bone, round at one end, pointed at the other. Used for scoring and folding paper.

Broad-edged or square-edged (nib) Produces thick and thin strokes without pressure, when kept at a constant angle to the writing line.

Capital (cap) Majuscule or upper-case letter.

Centre Aligning text symmetrically, to be visually balanced, on a vertical line.

Complementary colour Each primary colour has a complementary colour made by mixing the other two primaries.

Composition See Layout, Paste-up.

Counter The space enclosed within a letter.

Cross bar A horizontal letter stroke.

Descender Part of the lower-case letter extending below the baseline.

Design See Layout.

Dummy A mock-up of a manuscript book.

Exemplar A model alphabet or piece of work for students to study.

Form An abbreviation of letterform, the actual shape of the letter.

Format The overall shape of a piece of work.

Gouache Opaque watercolour or body colour.

Hand Another way of describing a letter style.

Interlinear (line) space The space between two lines of writing, the measurement usually related to the *x*, or body height, of the letter.

Layout The arrangement of all the elements of a piece of work, i.e. heading, text, etc. within a given area. See also Paste-up.

Letterform The actual shape of the letters, e.g. round, compressed, extended, etc.

Ligature A stroke that links two letters.

Lower-case Small letters or minuscules.

Majuscule A capital or Upper-case letter.

Minuscule Small or lower-case letters, which may have ascenders or descenders.

Monoline Letters made with a single weight of line, the essence of the letterform. Also used to describe tools such as pencils and rollerball pens that always make the same width of stroke. See Skeleton letter.

Paste-up Assembly of all the cut-out elements of a piece of work, stuck onto paper to finalise the layout.

Primary colour A colour that cannot be made by mixing.

Ranged left Text aligned at the left-hand side.

Ranged right Text aligned at the right-hand side.

Resist A technique involving two materials that do not mix, e.g. wax and watercolour paint.

Sans serif A letterform without serifs.

Secondary colour Made by mixing equal amounts of two primary colours.

Serif The strokes that lead into or finish a letter. In monoline letters they are always made as separate pen strokes.

Shade Made by adding black or the complementary of any given colour, in graded amounts.

Skeleton letter A letter made with a single weight of line. See Monoline.

Stem The main vertical stroke of a letter.

Stroke A component part of a letter, made without lifting the pen from the paper.

Tertiary colour Made by mixing equal amounts of one primary and one secondary colour.

Tint (of a colour) Made by adding white to any colour of gouache. Can be achieved in watercolour by adding water only.

Tone (tonal value) Gradations of colour from light to dark.

Tooth A slight surface texture on paper, which stops the nib/pen from slipping.

Typeface The design of type used in printing.

Upper-case Capital letters or majuscules.

Watercolour Translucent, water-based colours.

Weight The relationship of pen nib width to the letter height. Can also be described as light, regular or bold.

Writing line The line on which letters are written. See also Baseline.

x **height** (typographical term) The body or main part of lower-case letters, not including ascenders and descenders.

Useful websites

Most of the materials used in this book are easily found in stationers and art shops across the country. In case of difficulty in sourcing particular products, take a look at the websites in this list and contact the manufacturers direct for local stockists.

Pens, pencils and markers

Pilot Pen Company:
www.pilotpen.co.uk

Pentel: www.pentel.co.uk

Cumberland Pencil Company (Derwent Pencils):
www.pencils.co.uk/products/derwent

Artist's materials: paints, paper, brushes, etc.

Winsor & Newton:
www.winsornewton.com

Daler-Rowney:
www.daler-rowney.com

Pilot Pen Company:
www.pilotpen.co.uk

Specialist paper supplies, books on calligraphy

Falkiner Fine Papers (part of the Shepherd Group):
www.falkiners.com

John Neal, Bookseller:
www.johnnealbooks.com

Specialist artist's materials:

L Cornelissen & Son:
www.cornelissen.com

John Neal, Bookseller:
www.johnnealbooks.com

Calligraphy societies

The societies listed here have an international membership, with regular newsletters or journals to keep members up to date; many of them have affiliated local groups. Use the internet to find out more about your own national or regional group or guild.

Calligraphy and Lettering Arts Society (CLAS):
www.clas.co.uk

Australian Society of Calligraphers Inc.:
www.australiansocietyof calligraphers.com.au

New Zealand Calligraphers:
www.nzcalligraphers.co.nz

Society of Scribes (USA):
www.societyofscribes.org

Society of Scribes and Illuminators (UK):
www.calligraphyonline.org

Further reading

If you have enjoyed using this book and have been fired with enthusiasm to learn more about the craft of calligraphy, its history, techniques and materials, here are some useful titles to look for:

Calligraphy

The Beginner's Guide to Calligraphy, Margaret Morgan, New Holland Publishers (UK) Ltd, 2005.

Calligraphy Alphabets for Beginners, Janet Mehigan & Mary Noble, A & C Black 2008.

Step-by-step calligraphy, Susan Hufton, Sterling Publishing, 1997.

History, traditional techniques & materials

Illuminated Letters: A treasury of decorative calligraphy, Margaret Morgan, A&C Black Publishers Ltd, 2006.

Historical Scripts: A handbook for calligraphers, Stan Knight, A&C Black Publishers Ltd, 1984.

(This book may be hard to find, so try Amazon, second-hand book-shops or websites and libraries.)

Colour mixing, choosing colours

Blue and Yellow Don't Make Green, Michael Wilcox, School of Colour Publishing, 1991.

The Artist's Guide to Selecting Colours, Michael Wilcox, School of Colour Publishing, 1997.

INDEX

alphabet 12, 14, 28, 34, 43
alignment 78-82

backgrounds 8, 86-9
binding 8, 90-92
book 8
brushes 45, 47

calligraphy markers 45
capitals
    compressed 6, 28-33, 62,
    63, 66-9
    extended 34-37, 64
    monoline
        classic 12-15, 62,
        63
        Roman 8, 12-37
    slanted 30
colour 9, 24, 26, 33, 43-50, 66, 81,
    84-9
combinations 22, 63, 64
composition 70
construction 12-13, 29, 35, 38
contrast 27, 63, 71, 77, 79
crayons, wax 9
cross-bar variations 30, 66

design 70-82
drawing board 10

emphasis 27, 33, 77, 79
eraser 9
exercises 8, 16-18, 23-27, 31, 32,
    33, 36, 49, 50, 63-9, 71, 84
experimenting 62, 70-1,
extremes 63

family groups 12-13, 17, 30, 31,
    36, 38
form 43, 65
freeform 66-9

gel markers 45, 61

italicising (see slanting)

inks 44, 45, 47
    Japanese ink 44

layering 62, 72-3
letters
    capitals (see capitals)
    extended 6, 65
    height 26
    lower-case 38-44
        classic 39
        compressed 40, 44
        extended 41
        serifs 42
    modified 6
light 10
lines 21, 66
linking 22, 30, 33

materials 9, 10, 45-7,
mixing palettes 45

overflow 26

paints 46, 49, 50, 60, 81, 84
    gouache 8, 45, 46, 56-7, 69
    mixing 84-5
    stencil 47
    watercolour 8, 45, 46, 87-9
papers 9, 10, 45, 47, 50
paste-up layout 80-82
patterns 18, 42, 63
pencils 8, 9, 11, 15, 45
    clutch 9, 15
    graphite 9
pens 9, 45-7, 51-9
    bamboo 59
    cola 8, 52-5, 67, 69
    fountain 45
    edged 15, 45
    grip 16
    marker 9
    monoline dip-nibs 45
    nibs 6, 45, 46, 47, 52
    ornament 45
plastic drinking straw 58

rollerball 9, 43
Script 45
string 56
wax resist 59
planning 76-82
plotting 17, 20
position 17
pressure 17
proportions 29, 31

revisions 25
ruler (see tools)
ruling up 11, 16, 17, 18, 24, 32, 81

serifs 22-3, 30, 32, 35, 42, 43
shadow 8
sitting 10
skeleton letters (see capitals:
    monoline)
slanting 30
spacing 29, 30, 31, 32, 33, 36, 37,
    43, 77
    letters 17, 19, 20, 23, 32
    words and lines 21, 23, 25,
    26, 37
strokes 13, 14, 15, 16, 31, 35, 36,
    38, 39, 42

template 11, 24, 81
texture 18, 25, 26, 27, 33, 63
tools 9, 45-7
ruler 9, 11, 45
T-square 11

words 23
working surface 10